HORRIBLE H

CRACKIN'
CASTLES

erry Deary Illustrated by **Martin Brown**

SCHOLASTIC

Scholastic Children's Books,
Euston House, 24 Eversholt Street,
London NW1 1DB, UK

A division of Scholastic Ltd
London ~ New York ~ Toronto ~ Sydney ~ Auckland
Mexico City ~ New Delhi ~ Hong Kong

Published in the UK by Scholastic Ltd, 2016

Text © Terry Deary, 2016
Illustrations © Martin Brown, 2016
Cover line and colour by Rob Davis

ISBN 978 1407 16633 9

Printed in Great Britain by CPI Group (UK) Ltd, Croydon CR0 4YY

6 8 10 9 7 5

CONTENTS

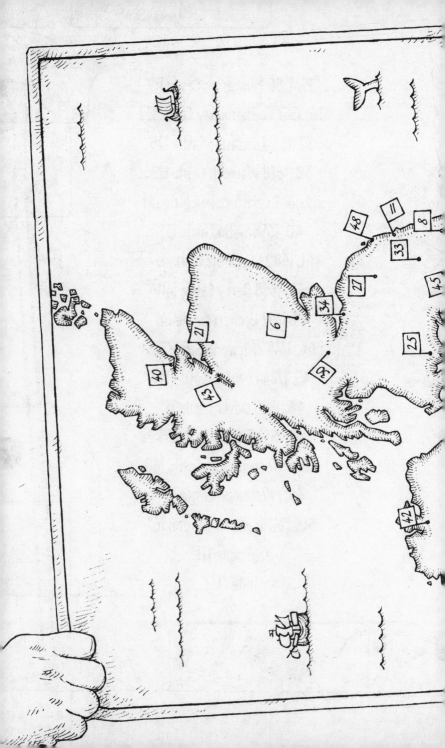

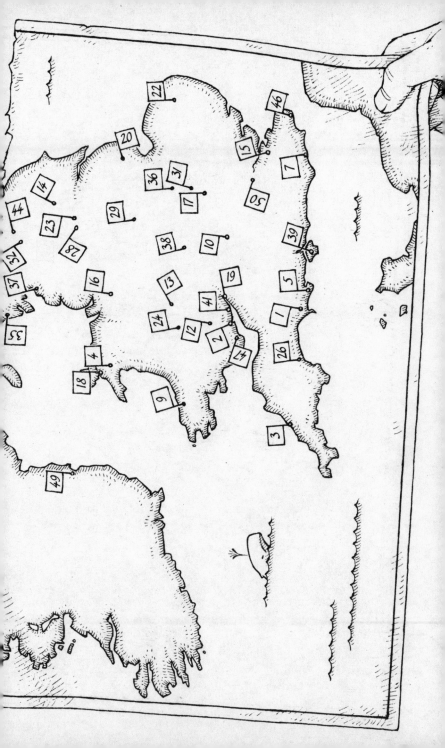

INTRODUCTION

Imagine you are a peasant. You know the sort of thing ... you're smelly with rotten teeth, always hungry and so poor you couldn't even afford a mobile phone. (But as they haven't been invented that doesn't bother you so much.)

You have to work hard for your dirty, damp, draughty house and putrid, pukesome, pathetic food, then you have to pay taxes to the church and taxes to your lord. If he gets into an argument with another lord then he'll force you to fight for him (if you're a bloke).

Yes, you have to risk your life for some posh bloke who isn't as smelly as you, has nicer teeth and doesn't go hungry. If mobile phones had been invented he'd have one in every room. Don't you just hate him?

Ooooh, but it makes you angry. If all you peasants got together you could attack his lordship and share out all his money. But, if you did, you know his son would just take over.

IT'S KNIGHT AFTER KNIGHT AFTER KNIGHT

And you can't fight him on horseback because you don't have a horse. *He* does and he can ride you down.

Plus he has a castle. He can hide inside its walls, of course … but *you*, dear peasant, could wait till it's dark and use ladders to surprise him.

Why don't you give it a go?

Well the first thing you rebels will see as you shamble up the hill is the castle. And you stop. It is so very B-I-G. A man who can build a fortress like that must be a powerful and scary man. Even if he's as weak as milky tea his castle makes him LOOK strong.

The man inside may be about as strong as a wet lettuce leaf but he isn't daft. He KNOWS a great castle makes him scary.

A lot of castles were built to defend a lord's land. Many were never attacked and defended. But their main use was to look forbidding and menacing. They were there to scare peasants like you. If you ever felt like rebelling you'd take one look at the castle and go home to your miserable, flea-ridden straw bed in your rat-infested hovel.

Most castles are gone to ruin these days. Yet their broken and ruined towers and walls still look creepsome. We visit them to wonder at the long-forgotten builders and listen to the long-remembered tales they have to tell. Many are horrible tales of blood and butchery, torture and terror, death ... and dung.

Here are the top 50. But be warned. Some are so scary you may want to read them with your eyes closed.

1. MAIDEN CASTLE
AD 43

This is Britain's oldest and biggest fortress. The Britons of the Iron Age dug a circular ditch around a hilltop and piled up a mound. (Mounds around are called 'ramparts'.) If an enemy attacked then the ramparts slowed them down. The defenders battered any attacker with stones fired from slings.

Terrible Tale

In AD 43 the Romans arrived ... and showed just how feeble mighty hillforts like Maiden Castle really were. They captured them one after another. The Brits stood on the ramparts to drive them back. The Romans had a machine that fired hundreds of iron-tipped arrows. The defenders hid or ran away ... wouldn't you?

Many of the British tribes surrendered to the Romans. But in North West London were the Catuvellauni tribe led by Togodumnus and Caratacus. They decided to stand and fight. The Romans shot the Brit warriors' horses from under them. Togodumnus was killed. Sensible Caratacus ran away to fight another day.

Did you know?

There's not a lot of burial at ancient British hillforts. Why not?

* The Brits probably took all the flesh off the corpse
* OR left the flesh to rot away
* OR let the flesh be eaten away by wild animals.

Then the bones were carried away. Do NOT try this on your teacher ... at least not while they're still alive.

The Legend

An archaeologist said that the Romans attacked Maiden Castle and butchered the men, women and children. A dozen corpses of chopped chaps, chapesses and children have been dug up. But they may not have died there. Not many people believe this story now.

2. CAERLEON FORT
AD 75

The Romans drove the British west to Wales and built camps – 'chesters' – at strong places along the way. In South Wales, in AD 75 they built Caerleon. It wasn't just a defence against the Wild Welsh. There was comfort and fun for the Roman soldiers with hot baths and an arena where gladiators fought wild animals to the death.

Terrible Tale

Caratacus had run away from his tribe in England. He began to stir up the Silures tribe down in South Wales. He attacked Roman supply wagons to feed his army. But some neighbouring tribes had made friends with the Romans – tribes like the Dobunni. So Caratacus robbed and murdered them too. He was one of the first Welsh heroes – even though he wasn't Welsh.

Did you know?

There is a stone carved at Caerleon – a prayer to the two Roman rulers of Britain, Caracalla and Geta. But the name of Geta has been hacked out. Why? Because the brothers fell out. The brothers had gone back to Rome where they divided the Emperor's palace in half and blocked up any doorways between the two parts. On 25 December AD 211 Caracalla said, 'Let's meet in my half of the palace.' His brother Geta was greeted by soldiers who butchered him. Their mother had come to keep the peace and Geta died in her arms – he was always her favourite.

Caracalla said…

Caracalla set about exterminating all of Geta's supporters – some reports claim 12,000 were slaughtered.

The Legend

The emperor Caracalla stopped on a journey to have a pee in a ditch. One of his guards lunged forward and killed Caracalla with a single blow. He was 'caught with his pants down' – or his toga up.

And Caratacus? He begged the queen of another tribe to shelter him. She had him bound in chains and handed him over to her friends … the Romans.

3. TINTAGEL CASTLE
AD 410

In AD 410 the Romans left Britain to defend Rome and never came back. The Celts ruled and built their own fortresses ... places like Tintagel in the west. It was nothing special till a monk called Geoffrey of Monmouth wrote a history of Britain and claimed that King Arthur was born there.

Terrible Tale

The old stories say Arthur protects Britain from danger. Some of the dangers are human, but many are ghastly and ghostly. He fights giant cat-monsters, terrible boars, dragons, warriors with the heads of dogs, giants, and witches.

YES, BUT NOT ALL AT THE SAME TIME

Tintagel Castle in Cornwall is on a bleak point
in the Atlantic, but could have been built there
to guard a harbour where foreign ships landed
with rich goods to trade.

There was some sort of fort on the rock in Roman
times. When Geoffrey of Monmouth said Arthur was
born on that spot, the local people went and built
a castle there. Now the legend of Arthur draws
almost 200,000 tourists to Tintagel every year.

It was quite useless when it was built. But
in 1588 the Spanish Armada was sailing to invade
Britain and it made a good lookout point.

The Legend

King Arthur STILL guards Britain. In a secret cave he lies
asleep with his knights. When Britain is in danger he will
wake up and save the country.

Underneath Tintagel Castle there is a cave where the
king's friend, Merlin the Magician, is said to live to this day.

MEOW

4. DINAS EMRYS FORT
450

Merlin is also said to have been in the mountains of Wales. The Romans had gone but the new invaders of England were the Savage Saxons. That's why Brit King Vortigern had to run away and build a fortress in Wales – Dinas Emrys.

Terrible Tale

BUT EVERY NIGHT WHEN THE WORK STOPPED...

OH NO, ME TOWER FELL DOWN. GET IT BUILT UP AGAIN LADS

BUT EVERY TIME IT WAS BUILT BY DAY, IT FELL BY NIGHT

WHUMP!

AFTER A COUPLE OF WEEKS VORTIGERN DECIDED TO ASK A WISE OLD MAN TO HELP...

SO, WHY DOES MY TOWER KEEP FALLING DOWN?

AN OLD WELSH CUSTOM SAYS A NEW HOUSE MUST HAVE A BLOOD SACRIFICE. SOMETIMES A HUMAN VICTIM IS WALLED UP ALIVE

NASTY

SOMETIMES THEY ARE KILLED AND THEIR BLOOD MIXED WITH THE CEMENT. BUT THE BLOOD MUST BE THE BLOOD OF AN INNOCENT FATHERLESS BOY

RIGHT LADS, FIND ME AN INNOCENT FATHERLESS BOY

VORTIGERN'S MEN BROUGHT BACK YOUNG MERLIN — THE BOY WHO WOULD GROW TO BE A FAMOUS MAGICIAN

RIGHT LADS, GIVE HIM THE CHOP

NO, WAIT, DON'T KILL ME. KILLING ME WILL NOT STOP YOUR CASTLE FALLING DOWN. HE'S A STUPID WISE MAN

21

LISTEN. BENEATH THIS GROUND THERE IS A POOL. AND IN THE POOL THERE ARE TWO DRAGONS, ONE RED AND ONE WHITE. EVERY NIGHT THEY FIGHT AND THAT'S WHAT BRINGS THE TOWER DOWN

SO, WHAT CAN WE DO ABOUT IT?

THE RED DRAGON IS WALES, THE WHITE DRAGON IS SAXON ENGLAND. WHEN THE RED DRAGON DEFEATS THE WHITE THEN PEACE WILL RETURN

OH, SO ALL WE HAVE TO DO IS DEFEAT THE SAXONS. RIGHT LADS, OFF TO FIGHT THE SAXONS...

Did you know?

The British really did defeat the Saxons in battles at that time – and when Dinas Emrys was dug up in the 1950s they really did find a deep pool.

The Legend

Before Merlin left he buried a cauldron full of gold beneath Dinas Emrys. Over the mouth of the cave he rolled a huge stone, which he covered up with earth and green turf, so that it is impossible for anyone to find it. This treasure was meant for some special person in a future generation. This special person will be a youth with yellow hair and blue eyes.

5. CORFE CASTLE
978

The Saxons defeated the British and ruled England. But the Vikings invaded and took over the North-eastern half of England. It was known as Danelaw ... because the Danish Vikings made the laws. King Alfred the Great made peace with them, but then he died – which was a big mistake. That left the Saxons to squabble over his kingdom in the south – Wessex.

Terrible Tale

Edgar had been a strong ruler but, like Alfred, he did a stupid thing and died. He was just 32 and his son, Edward, was about 13 when he took the throne, poor lad. Then HE died just three years later at Corfe Castle. If there had been newspapers in his day they may have reported his death ...

THE SAXON Sun

FREE RUBBISH
WITH OUR DOUBLE YOUR GARBAGE OFFER

18 March 978

EDWARD DEADED

Unpopular Ed

Young King Edward died at Corfe Castle today. He was about fifteen years old and had enemies for all of his short reign. The enemies said he was too young, yet they have replaced him with his brother Ethelred the Unready who is only ten. *The Saxon Sun* asks, 'If Eddie wasn't ready then how could Unready be ready?' (If you see what we mean.) The bad-tempered King Ed was visiting Ethelred in Corfe Castle when the death happened.

Ethelred's ministers were waiting for the king and, as he started to get down from his horse, they stabbed him to death then tried to burn the body.

Some reports say the king's mother watched her son being murdered. Others say she was one of the killers. Ethelred has already said he will take the crown but will not punish the killers.

WHAT OUR SAXON CELEBRITIES SAID ABOUT ED. PAGES 3 TO 42

Ethelred went on to be one of Britain's worst kings. He tried to pay the Vikings to go away - giving them gold weighing 10,000 kilos in the year 991 - so they kept coming back. Who can blame them?

The Legend

Chronicles said 'A cloud as red as blood' was seen after Ethelred was crowned – it appeared at midnight and vanished at dawn – it was a sign that God was angry. King Edward's body was thrown into a swamp. It didn't sink – a miracle. Edward (the vicious and cruel lad) became a saint. But a dead one, of course.

WHERE'S IT GONE?

6. DUNSINANE CASTLE
1054

The Viking King Canute ruled all of England and made Scotland obey him too. Duncan became Scottish king and in 1039 and marched south to attack England. When he reached Durham his army was beaten, thumped and thrashed. Oh dear. That did not make him popular back home in Scotland so his cousin, Lord Macbeth, met him in battle and Duncan was killed. Macbeth became king in 1040.

Terrible Tale

In 1054 Macbeth was attacked by an army of English, Vikings and the Scottish prince Malcolm. Macbeth was beaten at Dunsinane Castle and had to give up a lot of his land to Malcolm.

How do you defeat a king in his castle? 550 years later the writer William Shakespeare turned Macbeth's story into a play ... though Shakespeare got a lot of his facts wrong because he hadn't read his *Horrible Histories* books.

Shakespeare's play says Macbeth met three witches who told him his future. They said:

MACBETH SHALL NEVER VANQUISHED BE, UNTIL GREAT BIRNAM WOOD TO HIGH DUNSINANE SHALL COME AGAINST HIM

CRIKEY

Macbeth thought he was safe. Birnam Wood could never march against him … could it?

But (the play says) Malcolm's army cut down lots of branches and hid behind them as they crept towards Dunsinane Castle. The defenders (who must have been asleep or needed their eyes testing) didn't see them until it was too late and the castle was captured.

Now you know how to attack a castle. Use camouflage.

Malcolm was back 3 years later and met Macbeth in a battle in the north of Scotland and killed him.

Did you know?

'Dunsinane' means 'hill of ants'. Would you like to live on top of an anthill?

The Legend

If you want to make a magic spell, like Shakespeare's witches, then take a pot and boil up …

EYE OF NEWT AND TOE OF FROG, WOOL OF BAT AND TONGUE OF DOG, ADDER'S FORK AND BLIND-WORM'S STING, LIZARD'S LEG AND HOWLET'S WING

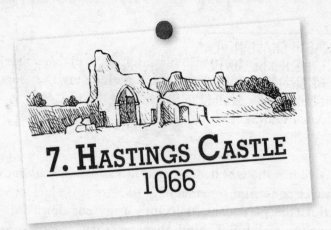

7. HASTINGS CASTLE
1066

The Vikings moved south and grabbed land in the north of France where they were known as the 'North Men' ... or 'Norman' for short. The Normans were great castle builders ... they needed to be because nobody liked them much. In 1066 their leader, William the Conqueror, landed on the south coast of England and defeated the English King Harold at the Battle of Hastings.

Terrible Tale

When the Normans landed near Hastings they found the Saxons waiting for them at the top of Senlac Hill. The knights weren't very keen on charging up the hill ... the Saxons were big blokes with swords and battle-axes and the poor Normans could get hurt.

I'M NOT AFRAID OF DEATH, I JUST DON'T WANT TO BE THERE WHEN IT HAPPENS

There is a legend (which may even be true) that a juggler called Taillefer told them there was nothing to worry about. He rode in front of the English army and sang a song about a French hero ... and juggled his sword at the same time. Clever chap.

That annoyed an English knight who rode out to attack him. Taillefer killed him. He then led William the Conqueror's troops into the Battle of Hastings. The Norman historian, Wace, said …

A minstrel named Taillefer went in front of the Norman army, singing and juggling with his sword while the troops marched behind singing the Song of Roland.

WATCH THE EARS, MATE

Brave chap. He was swallowed up by the English army and hacked to pieces. Dead brave.

Did you know?

Hastings was the first castle the Normans built on
English soil. But it was made in France. The Normans
carried the pieces across the English Channel and
put the kit bits together when they landed.

William the Conqueror became king and dished
out England to his knights. They spread out and
started ruling their lands. The great age of
castle-building had begun. The first ones were
made of wood but in time they were replaced
with stone.

The Legend

A ghostly image of Hastings Castle can be seen floating
above the sea, with flags flying just as they would have
hundreds of years ago.

8. DURHAM CASTLE
1069

The Normans didn't rule England without a struggle. William the Conqueror gave the job of ruling Durham to the Earl of Northumberland, Robert Comyn, who began to build his castle near the cathedral. He was a ruthless man and the Durham people feared for their lives. It was kill or be killed.

Terrible Tale

Simeon, a monk of Durham, reported:

The bishop of Durham told the earl, Robert Comyn, to stay away because rebels wanted to kill him. Comyn ignored the advice and entered Durham with seven hundred men, determined to punish the rebels. Any man who raised a weapon against a Norman was butchered.

BRUTAL

Then, very early on the morning of 31 January, the rebels broke in through all the gates, and running through the city hither and thither they killed the earl's men. So many were killed that every street was covered with blood, and filled with bodies. The blood that flowed in the streets was frozen by the bitter January winds.

COLD

The earl himself held out in a house near Palace Green so the rebels set it on fire. Of those persons who were within it some were burnt and some were slaughtered as soon as they stepped outside. The earl was put to death along with all of his followers, except for one, who escaped wounded.

LUCKY

Did you know?

King William waited till September. His avenging force reached Northallerton, north of York ... then were turned back by a miracle (the Durham people said). The Norman army marched into a thick fog (sent by God probably). The Normans panicked and turned back. Durham was saved.

But the truth is an invading Danish army landed on the Yorkshire coast – the Normans turned back to deal with the invaders first. Durham had not been saved for long.

William didn't just want to defeat the north – he wanted to destroy it. Every building his soldiers came across was burned. Every animal was killed so there was nothing left for the people to eat. Every man and boy they found was hacked to death – their corpses were left to rot by the side of the roads. The starving survivors were so desperate they ate the corpses to stay alive. William's ruthless revenge was known as 'The Harrying of the North'.

The north was like a desert. The towns and villages were still struggling to recover twenty years later. The north certainly didn't revolt again. The Conqueror's cruelty worked.

Yet there's a curious story that, twenty years after the destruction as William lay dying, the king said he was sorry it had happened.

The Legend

Simeon wrote:

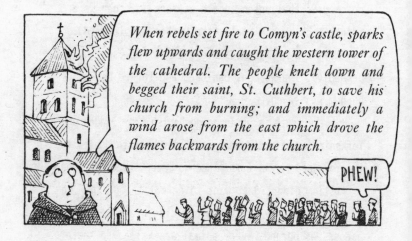

When rebels set fire to Comyn's castle, sparks flew upwards and caught the western tower of the cathedral. The people knelt down and begged their saint, St. Cuthbert, to save his church from burning; and immediately a wind arose from the east which drove the flames backwards from the church.

PHEW!

9. CILGERRAN CASTLE
1109

The Normans spread west and began to conquer Wales. Some of the princes there made peace and married into Norman families. William the Conqueror died in 1087. Welsh princes like Rhys ap Tewdwr were defeated – and he had his head lopped off. Rhys's head was still rolling on the ground when his daughter, Nest, married a Norman lord, Gerald of Windsor. Nest was a Welsh princess who was famous for her beauty.

Terrible Tale

OWAIN'S BAND CLIMBED THE WALLS AND ENTERED THE CASTLE WHILE THE GUARDS SLEPT. THEY SET FIRE TO SOME BUILDINGS AND GERALD WOKE UP

HE SNATCHED HIS SWORD AND RUSHED OUT...

NO. HE PANICKED. HE DIDN'T KNOW WHAT TO DO. SO NEST SAID, "DON'T GO OUT, MY LOVE; FOLLOW ME." AND SHE LED HIM TO A LITTLE ROOM...

YOU MEAN THE TOILET?

TOILETS IN THOSE DAYS WERE HOLES ON THE WALLS THAT YOU SAT ON AND LET EVERYTHING FALL INTO THE DITCH OUTSIDE

OH, THAT IS SÓ GROSS

ANYWAY, NEST STUFFED HER HUSBAND DOWN THE TOILET HOLE AND HE ESCAPED

POOR NEST MUST HAVE BEEN SO MISERABLE

NOT EXACTLY. SOME PEOPLE SAY SHE WENT OFF WITH HIM QUITE HAPPILY

THAT IS SO SHOCKING

The Legend

Nest wasn't too heartbroken when Owain was killed. She found other boyfriends. She ended up as the girlfriend of King Henry I of England – the man who had married her off to Gerald.

10. OXFORD CASTLE
1142

Henry I was on the throne and when he died he wanted his daughter, Empress Matilda, to be the next ruler. But most of the English lords wanted her cousin Stephen as king ... just because he was a bloke. How unfair is that? Stephen and Matilda's armies fought each other for the English throne and in the wars that followed the big losers were the people of England.

Terrible Tale

In 1142, during the wars, Matilda found herself trapped in Oxford Castle. Oxford was a tough town to attack, protected by its walls and by the River Isis, but Stephen led a sudden raid across the river. He led the charge and swam part of the way. Once on the other side, the king and his men stormed into the town, trapping the empress in the castle.

Stephen had to settle in for a long siege. Matilda was surrounded with no way out and no food getting in. There are TWO stories about what happened next:

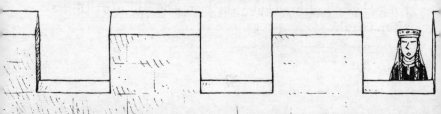

1 Just before Christmas, the Empress Matilda sneaked out of the castle gate with a handful of knights, crossed the icy river on foot and made her escape past the royal army to safety at Wallingford.

2 Another story says Matilda waited until the Castle Mill Stream was frozen over and then dressed in white as camouflage in the snow. She was lowered down the walls with three or four knights, leaving the castle defenders free to surrender the next day.

Did you know?

Stephen and Matilda did the arguing ... but the fighting and the dying was done by the peasants. And, while they were fighting, there was no one to care for the crops so the families went hungry. No wonder a monk wrote ...

I know not how to tell of all the cruelties they brought upon the people of this unhappy country. And so it lasted for nineteen years while Stephen was king, till the land was all undone and darkened with such deeds. Men said openly that Christ and his angels slept.

The Legend

A year before her Oxford escape, Matilda had made a similar one from being trapped in Devizes. She played dead. Matilda was dressed up in grave clothes like a corpse waiting to be buried. She was tied to a stretcher and the body was taken past the guards. Once the funeral party was well clear of Devizes the corpse sat up and laughed.

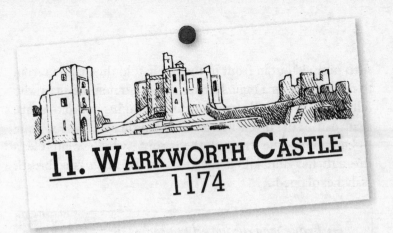

11. WARKWORTH CASTLE
1174

Matilda's son Henry II took the throne and is remembered for ordering the death of Thomas Becket, the Archbishop of Canterbury. Four of Henry's knights chopped Becket down in the cathedral and his brains flowed over the floor. Henry seemed cursed with bad luck. He had a wife (Eleanor) and sons (Henry, Geoffrey, Richard and John) who went to war with him. Then there were the Scots who kept raiding the north and attacking castles like Warkworth.

Terrible Tale

Bertram de Bothal fell in love with Isabel Widdrington of Northumberland. She promised to visit him but, after a week, she hadn't arrived. Bertram set out to find her.

Bertram learned that Isabel was being held prisoner in a Scottish castle and hurried find her. He watched the castle in secret. On the second night he saw a woman climbing down a rope from the tower and a man dressed in tartan helping her. It was his beloved Isabel.

Bertram followed the couple away from the castle and

then jumped out in front of them. He told the man in tartan to release her. In a rage, Bertram struck out at the man who fell to the ground. Barmy Bertram raised his sword to strike again but Isabel threw herself between them.

Of course she copped the sword, which went clean through her and killed the man. With her dying breath Isabel explained ...

Heartbroken Bert returned to Northumberland where he was granted sanctuary by Lord Percy at Warkworth Castle. The killer gave up all his wealth and left the castle to build the hermitage nearby. He carved a small chapel out of the rock face and spent years in prayer until his death. The ghost of Bertram de Bothal still haunts the hermit cave and castle.

The first Warkworth Castle, made of wood, was so feeble that when the Scots arrived in 1174 the people chose to hide in the church instead. Twenty years later Robert FitzRoger owned the castle and started building the strong stone walls you can see today.

Sir Henry Percy ruled the North when Henry IV was on the throne and lived at Warkworth. He was known as Harry Hotspur. Warkworth Castle and Hotspur are famous for being part of the action of Shakespeare's plays about Henry IV.

The Legend

Harry Hotspur was killed when he raised the visor on his armour helmet and was shot in the mouth by an arrow. His head was cut off and stuck on a pole over York City walls. Visitors to Warkworth say they've seen a grey lady in one of the towers. This is said to be the ghost of Margaret Neville – Harry Hotspur's mother. You will find there are a lot of grey or white ladies haunting castles. They should get together and form a club. As you wander the walls don't be surprised to spot the ghost of a young man running alongside you. Could it be Harry looking for his head?

HARD TO SPOT YOUR MISSING HEAD WHEN YOUR EYES ARE IN YOUR MISSING HEAD

12. ABERGAVENNY CASTLE
1175

In 1175 one of the nastiest Norman deeds was done at Abergavenny Castle. The Norman lord, William de Braose, was having a feast. A Christmas feast. How jolly? Not in the golden age of castles ...

Terrible Tale

William de Braose invited the Welsh chieftain of Gwent, Seisyll ap Dyfnwal, for Christmas dinner. How kind. Especially as it was Seisyll who had murdered William de Braose's Uncle Henry.

William had a very special Christmas present for Seisyll. If there had been newspapers in those days then it would have made the front page.

26 December 1175

The Abergavenny Advertiser

¹/₁₇ penny

SILENT KNIGHTS

'Tis the season to be jolly or … in the case of William de Braose … jolly vicious.

Our Norman lord sent out invitations to his old Welsh enemy, Seisyll, the chieftain of Gwent.

'Bring your brother-in-law, Gruffydd, and your top knights,' wily William wrote. 'We'll have a great knight out,' he joked.

The Welsh arrived and took off their weapons – it's good

WILLIAM AND FRIENDS WELCOME WELSH GUESTS

45

they started drinking and eating. A servant at Abergavenny Castle said this morning, 'There was more drinking than eating. Well, to tell the truth it was the Welsh doing all the drinking – William and the Normans just sipped a little watered wine.'

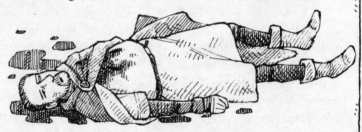

As midnight struck so did the Normans. First Lord William told his guests, 'I have made a new law that says no Welsh man will ever be allowed to carry a weapon in my lands again.'

Seisyll cried, 'You can never make us obey that, de Braose,' and that's just what the nifty Norman was waiting to hear.

'You've just refused to obey an order from the king,' William roared. 'That's treason. The punishment is death. Normans, kill them.'

That's when the Normans drew their weapons and hacked Seisyll and his knights to pieces. The only Christmas boxes they'll be getting are wooden boxes to bury them in.

But William's revenge was not complete. William went after Seisyll's wife Gwladus as she tried to escape.

She tried to shield her seven-year-old son in her arms. They were both hacked to death.

'Blood all over the rushes on the floor,' our servant said. 'Blood and body bits. We'll have to throw out all the rushes and bury the bodies. We was hoping for a holiday. Some Christmas this has turned out to be.

William de Braose became known as the 'Ogre of Abergavenny'.

In 1246 Eva de Braose of Abergavenny had a pet squirrel that she adored. One day the squirrel scampered over the castle wall. Eva tried to recover it ... she fell to her death.

The Legend

Matilda of Hay was married to William (the 'Ogre of Abergavenny'.) The local Welsh people thought Matilda had powers of witchcraft. As if by magic she told King John she knew he had murdered his nephew Arthur. Big mistake, Matilda. John had her arrested along with her son, William, and imprisoned in Windsor Castle. They were later walled up, alive, in a cell at Corfe Castle with just a piece of raw bacon and a sheaf of wheat. They were both found dead after 11 days.

13. LUDLOW CASTLE
1190

Castles were the home of Norman knights, but the knights were often away fighting in the Holy Land ... wars known as 'The Crusades'. Between 1096 and 1272 there were nine Crusades to choose from so it was never boring. There was also the idea that knights should behave like gentlemen – 'chivalry'. But not all knights were chivalrous, as their victims found out.

Terrible Tale

"Women?' The young knight, Geoffrey, laughed and the sound echoed round the cold stone walls of the dungeon cell. 'They love me. And who can blame them. I'm handsome, strong and brave. Any woman would be proud to be my love.'

The rat twitched his whiskers and scuttled back to its nest under the straw. 'You don't appear to believe me, Master Rat,' the young man said. 'I'll bet you a piece of stale bread that I'll be out of here within a week.'

Geoffrey turned his head sharply as he heard the rattle of keys in the lock of the cell. He brushed the straw off his jerkin, sat up straight and fixed a smile upon his face. The door swung open and the girl hurried in with a dish of gruel and a mug of ale. Her nose curled back at the smell in the filthy air and she placed the food carefully on the floor. It was the only time she would come within reach of the chained man. Suddenly his chain clattered, his hand shot out and grabbed her wrist.

'Ah,' she cried.

'Hush,' he said quickly. 'Stay just a few moments, Marion,' he went on softly.

'My father will be suspicious,' she said anxiously.

Geoffrey spoke quickly and didn't release his grip on the girl's wrist. 'Yesterday, after you'd gone, his lordship came to see me. He has given me just three days to talk. He wants me to tell him our plans for capturing Ludlow Castle. I would not betray my friends, of course.'

'And after three days?' she asked.

'After three days he will torture me. First he will use hot irons on my face . . .'

'No,' she gasped.

'I can bear the pain,' the young man shrugged, 'But it may spoil my looks. No maiden would marry me with those scars. Or he may gouge out my eyes . . .'

'No,' she gasped. 'His lordship's not a cruel man.'

The prisoner shrugged one shoulder. 'We'll see . . . at least you'll see. I won't have any eyes left to see.'

'How can you joke about such a thing?' she asked.

'True. I'd be sad to lose my eyes. I'd never be able to see a beautiful face again. A beautiful face like yours.'

The girl blushed and tore her wrist away from his grip. She hurried from the cell and closed the door. The young man smiled.

The next day she came in and knelt beside him silently. She took a small key from her belt and unfastened the chains that bound his wrists. She slipped a larger key from the ring and pressed it into his hand. 'The key to the outer door,' she muttered. 'Let yourself out.'

He touched her hand softly. 'Thank you, Marion. You have saved me and I owe you my life. The only way I can repay my debt is by marrying you.'

The girl looked up, startled. 'You'll take me with you?'

'Ah,' he whispered. 'Not just yet. I need time to get away. I want you to stay here, to cover for my escape as long as you can. I'll return for you a week today. Listen, here's what we'll do . . .'

That night, as the monastery bell tolled midnight, he

slipped away from the moon-shadows of the castle and stole a horse from the village below. Within an hour he was ten miles from Ludlow. A week later he was back, as he had promised.

A ladder hung from the window as he knew it would. It was made of strong leather rope and led up to a window in the west tower. A window that wasn't overlooked by the patrolling guards.

Geoffrey climbed it swiftly and felt Marion's strong hands grasp his wrists and pull him over the stone sill. A candle lit the room and glinted on the knight's excited eyes. Marion gave him a nervous smile and moved towards the window. 'Where are you going?' he asked.

'Down the ladder. Away with you,' she said.

He shook his head. 'We have one or two visitors who want to climb that ladder first,' Geoffrey grinned.

'Visitors?'

'Friends of mine. Friends who want a little revenge on your lord.'

A man's face appeared at the window ledge. Geoffrey pulled him into the room. That man in turn helped a second, then a third. In five minutes the room was crowded with hard-faced, leather-jacketed men with soft boots and cruel knives.

'What are you doing?' the bewildered girl asked.

Geoffrey ignored her. Instead he turned his back on her and spoke to the men. 'Kill the guards, throw their bodies over the walls then lower the drawbridge . . .'

'My father's on duty tonight!' Marion cried.

'Kill all the guards,' Geoffrey said slowly. 'Our troops will ride in and finish the job.'

Marion opened her mouth but before she could scream a warning the knight had clamped a rough, gloved hand over it. He held it suffocatingly tight until the last man had left the room and closed the door. 'Women are fools,' he sneered at her.

But while he held her mouth closed he couldn't control her arms. She had carefully slipped the dagger from his belt and turned it till the point was under his ribs. With all of her strength she pushed upwards.

His lips went tense and his eyes showed more surprise than pain. There was a soft gurgle in his throat as he fell back against the wall. He remained there for half a minute, clawing helplessly at the thing in his side before he slid slowly to the floor.

Marion hurried to the door and looked out onto the battlements. There were cries of terror as men struggled in the darkness and tumbled from their posts. The drawbridge dropped with a crash and there was the sound of horses clattering into the courtyard.

One man's voice seemed to rise above the other cries. 'We've been betrayed!' the voice wailed. 'Betrayed.'

Marion turned back to the room, walked past the lifeless knight and climbed onto the window ledge. 'Oh, we've all been betrayed,' she said dully. The girl simply leaned forward and let herself drop.

In the dark chaos of the night no one heard one more small cry, one more soft crunching of bone on rock.

Did you know?

Marion wasn't the only castle-dweller to be betrayed. A robber held in Haverfordwest Castle (Wales) became friends with some young squires who were training to be knights. He fixed arrowheads for them and gave them to the boys for their bows. The boys begged that the robber be allowed out for some fresh air - in their care. He took them hostage and used them to bargain for his freedom.

The Legend

Marion's ghost can be seen acting out this tragedy at Ludlow Castle, while visitors hear the sound of her lopped lover dying. 'Gurgle, burble, urk.'

14. YORK CASTLE
1190

The Crusades cost money. Kings would tax their subjects to pay the soldiers to fight their wars. When the money ran out they would borrow it. But it was against Christian law to lend money. The poor kings had to turn to the Jewish people to lend them money. And if you owe someone money you may end up hating them. That's what happened to the Jews in York.

Terrible Tale

Richard I, 'The Lionheart', was crowned in 1189. He banned all Jews from his coronation and when some dared to bring rich gifts to the palace he had them stripped, flogged and thrown out.

People said that Richard had ordered all English Jews to be killed … it wasn't true but people in London believed it. They burned down Jewish houses and attacked them.

Richard said it had to stop and he punished the attackers. But the next year he decided to fight in the Third Crusade. So he was away when the people of York decided to attack the city's Jews.

* Josce was the leader of York's Jewish citizens and he led the local families into the castle.
* They shut themselves away in the keep, known as Clifford's Tower. The mob surrounded the Tower.
* The Jewish priest, their religious leader Rabbi Yom Tov, told the Jewish people to kill themselves and their families, rather than be killed by the mob.
* Josce obeyed. He started it by slaying his wife Anna and his two children.
* The father of each family killed his wife and children, before Yom Tov and Josce set fire to the wooden tower, killing themselves.
* The few Jews who did not kill themselves died in the fire, or were murdered by rioters.
* 150 Jews died.

Did you know?

Richard died on a Crusade in 1199. He was walking around a castle under siege without his armour. Richard laughed at one defender who had a crossbow in one hand and a frying pan as a shield to beat off missiles. The man aimed at the king, which the king jeered at. But another crossbowman then struck the king in the left shoulder near the neck.

A surgeon known as 'The Butcher' tried to pull it out but mangled the king's arm. The wound turned poisonous. Richard asked to have the crossbowman brought before him; the man turned out to be a boy. This boy claimed that Richard had killed his father and two brothers, and that he, the boy, had shot at Richard in revenge. The boy expected to be executed, but Richard forgave him, saying,

> LIVE ON, AND BY MY KINDNESS LIVE TO SEE THE LIGHT OF ANOTHER DAY

He gave orders for the boy to be set free and sent away with 100 shillings. Richard died in the arms of his mother.

The young crossbowman was skinned alive and hanged as soon as Richard died.

The Legend

Richard's father, Henry II, died and his body was carried to the grave in an open coffin. His hated son, Richard I, arrived to meet the procession. As Richard leaned over the coffin blood spurted from the nose of his dead father. 'His angry ghost doesn't want his son there!' the watching people muttered.

15. ROCHESTER CASTLE
1215

King John argued with the church and with his barons. They forced him to sign a document called 'Magna Carta' – that's Latin for 'The Great Charter'. He gave away some of his powers. But John never meant to keep his side of the agreement and Rochester Castle became the centre of one of the nastiest terrors of his reign.

Terrible Tale

The barons broke the Magna Carta too. They were supposed to hand over Rochester Castle to John. Instead they entered it in early October and locked the gates. John was furious so he marched from London to besiege it.

His army had great war catapults and they began showering the castle keep and the walls with huge rocks. But with walls 4 metres thick, the keep held strong.

After a month John's army wrote to London and asked for…

FORTY OF THE FATTEST PIGS, THE SORT LEAST GOOD FOR EATING

In a world before gunpowder, pig fat was used as a fire-starter. First they dug a tunnel under the tower. Then they lit a pig-fat fire.

It made part of the castle collapse, but the keep was divided into two parts. The defenders just retreated to the half that wasn't damaged.

Still, it was grim for them inside. The soldiers were forced to kill their horses and eat them. (Neigh, it's true.)

Then the fighting men sent the weakest people out to save on food. Some reports say they had their hands and feet cut off by King John's men.

By the end of November the defenders finally gave up and were made prisoners. John wanted his attackers to kill all the defenders who had given them so much trouble. King John's men didn't do that. They said one day it might be their turn to be besieged and they didn't want mass killing to be a habit.

There was just one defender, an archer, who had once fought FOR the king then switched sides. They decided to hang him.

Did you know?

Ruthless John had captured his nephew, Arthur, and imprisoned him in Paris. John got drunk, killed Arthur, tied a stone round his body and threw the corpse in the River Seine.

The Legend

In 1264 the castle at Rochester was being defended by Ralph de Capo who was planning to marry Lady Blanche. One of the attackers was Sir Gilbert de Clare... a jealous man because Lady Blanche had turned him down.

Ralph de Capo left the castle with some of his men to drive off the attackers. Gilbert de Clare circled around and entered the castle dressed in a suit of armour looking just like the one worn by de Capo. (Sneaky or what?)

He caught up with Blanche on the battlements and grabbed her. She struggled to push de Clare away. Her lover, de Capo, came back in time to see her struggle. He was a great shot with a bow. He fired an arrow which hit de Clare but it bounced off his armour and went through the heart of Lady Blanche, killing her.

Her ghost, dressed in a white robe and still with the arrow through her heart, forever walks the battlements near the round tower. Awwww.

16. BEESTON CASTLE
1220

If you think eating horses at Rochester was sad (or saddle) then Beeston was just as bad. Ranulf de Blondeville built Beeston Castle when he returned from the Fifth Crusade around 1220.

Terrible Tale

To provide the castle's inhabitants with a supply of fresh water two wells were dug into the rock. One of them, 124m deep, is one of the deepest castle wells in England.

The story goes that Richard II hid bags and bags of gold somewhere in the castle – most likely in the deep well. As he was murdered soon after, no one ever knew where he'd put them. So these riches are still hidden to this day … if there are any there. Many people have tried to find the treasures of Beeston but failed.

A fairy-tale story, you may think. But secret passageways and tunnels have been uncovered inside the well, so something strange and mysterious must have happened there.

When Richard II was murdered, his enemy, Henry IV, found Richard's gold and jewellery in the places he'd hidden them. So maybe there never was any treasure at Beeston.

In the English Civil War in the 1640s the castle was captured by one side and then the other.

In 1643 the Royalist Captain Thomas Sandford and eight soldiers from that army crept into Beeston at night. The castle governor, Captain Thomas Steele, was so shocked by the crafty attack that he surrendered. His attackers spared his life... but Steele was shot by his own side for losing the castle.

The Legend

When King Charles I was captured, his Royalist troops surrendered Beeston one last time. They were in a terrible state. The last Royalists were so desperate for food that they were forced to eat castle cats. Nasty.

BUT WE SURVIVED. BY A WHISKER

The winners reported ...

There was neither meat, Ale nor Beer found in the castle. Only a piece of Turkey pie, two biscuits, and a pair of live peacocks.

Lucky peacocks.

17. BEDFORD CASTLE
1224

King John died in 1216 and his son Henry III reigned... and reigned... and reigned. In 1224 the baron Falkes de Breauté fell out with Henry III, and the king marched on Bedford Castle. Falkes had left the castle in the hands of his brother William, with 80 men to defend it.

Terrible Tale

Henry III's force may have been over 2,500 men who came from all over England to Bedford. Around 200 of them were killed. You can imagine that made the other 2,300 a bit cross.

They brought some catapults and built others outside the castle walls – one trebuchet and seven mangonels in all. With nearly 45,000 crossbow bolts they were ready to attack. The king arrived… with lots of fine food for himself and barrels of wine. He wasn't going to suffer like the defenders, was he?

William was sure his brother would arrive to save him so he held on. He even hoped the Pope would write to the king and order him to spare the castle.

The walls were battered – not like cod in a chip shop but with huge stones. Mines were dug under the walls and fires lit to make them crack and collapse. After an 8-week siege the women were released. The men surrendered the next day and the king's flag flew over the castle.

What would you do if you were Henry III?

a) Spare the women but not the men?
b) Copy his dad (King John) at Rochester and spare everyone except the traitors?
c) Kill them all?

Answer:
(a) The women were set free but the defenders were all hanged, even William de Breauté. And they said King John was cruel? Henry III was brutal … of should that be Breuté?

Did you know?

Two days after the men were executed the letter arrived from the Pope telling King Henry to stop his fight against the de Breautés. Too late. If only the Pope had had email. Or even a passing angel to deliver his message.

The Legend

Falkes de Breauté let his brother die defending Bedford. He was sure his castle could last for a year. He was shocked that it fell in 8 weeks. He begged the king to forgive him and he was spared. He had started the trouble that led to his brother and nearly 80 men being executed, yet he lived on. He was just exiled to France. So unfair.

18. CAERNARFON CASTLE
1301

I'M ED, YOU'RE DEAD

In 1282 Llywelyn ap Gruffydd, Prince of Wales, died. Wales was without a prince and they hated the English King Edward I. Big Ed started making the Welsh obey English laws. And in 1292 he charged them more tax than the English were paying. No wonder they rebelled ... again. In 1293 the Welsh rebels took the north-west of Wales – Gwynedd. Edward defeated them at Maes Maidog. A few days later 500 Welsh soldiers were sleeping. Edward's men massacred them in their sleep. Ed started building beautiful castles to keep the Welsh under control. Castles like Caernarfon.

Terrible Tale

Teachers for hundreds of years have told the story of how the first English Prince of Wales was crowned. Here is the teacher's side ... and here is how a true Welsh child might like to argue with it.

KING EDWARD CAME TO CAERNARFON. IT WAS SAID THAT IN 1300, WHEN HIS WIFE GAVE BIRTH TO A SON AT CAERNARFON CASTLE, THE KING CALLED THE BABY 'PRINCE OF WALES AND COUNT OF CHESTER'

NO, MISS. MY DAD SAYS THE PRINCE WAS BORN IN CAERNARFON IN 1284

I LOOKED IT UP ON THE INTERNET AND IT SAYS 1300. ANYWAY, THE PRINCE WAS BORN AND EDWARD SAID, 'PEOPLE OF WALES, HERE IS MY ELDEST SON...'

MY DAD SAYS ALFONSO WAS EDWARD'S ELDEST SON

BUT ALFONSO WASN'T BORN IN WALES. NOW THE WELSH PEOPLE WEREN'T SURE ABOUT AN ENGLISH PRINCE OF WALES, SO EDWARD DID A CLEVER THING. HE RAISED HIS SON ABOVE HIS HEAD...

HE'D HAVE A BIT OF A JOB – THE PRINCE WAS 17 YEARS OLD BY THEN!

The Welsh were NOT overjoyed and many are still not happy with an English Prince of Wales.

Even 600 years later, in 1911, there were Welsh people who hated the idea of an English Prince of Wales. In 1911 the Rhondda MP, Keir Hardie, said this when a new Prince of Wales was due to get the honour in a ceremony...

> *There is to be a ceremony to remind us that an English king and his robber barons tried for ages to destroy the Welsh people. They succeeded in robbing them of their lands and driving them to the mountains like hunted beasts. The ceremony ought to make every Welshman blush with shame.*

Not a fan of the English royal family then?

The Legend

Caernarfon Castle has a Floating Lady. This unusual ghost is sometimes seen drifting down the corridors, and meddles with any electrical stuff left out at night.

19. BERKELEY CASTLE
1327

Castles could be dark and secret places. They were handy spots for anyone who wanted to get away with murder. Edward I had been a fearsome warrior known as 'The Hammer of the Scots'. His son Edward II wasn't a keen soldier and lost the famous Battle of Bannockburn to the Scots. He preferred swimming and dressing up. He should have stayed away from Berkeley Castle.

Terrible Tale

Edward II's wife, Isabella, was one of the most evil of the Brit queens ever to rule. She wanted rid of the king (Edward II) so her son (Edward III) could take over the throne.

First she got her boyfriend, Roger Mortimer, to raise an army and attack King Edward. When Mortimer had captured the king, Isabella ordered Edward to be thrown in jail in Berkeley Castle. She wanted him dead, but didn't want it to look like he'd been murdered.

Underneath the jail the corpses of dead prisoners were left to rot. She hoped Ed would die from an infection. He didn't.

He was then left to starve. He didn't.

Isabella then sent a message to the jailers. It seemed a harmless enough message. In fact it was a code. It meant, 'Kill him.'

One story says jailers smothered the king with cushions then pushed a hot poker into his bowels from underneath.

Isabella gave Ed a lovely funeral and even went along herself. A poet called her 'The She-Wolf of France'.

Did you know?

Isabella had hated her husband and had him murdered, yet she was buried with his heart clutched to her chest - a sign of true love?

The Legend

Edward II died in such terrible agony that it has been said for many centuries his screams could be heard miles from the castle every 21 September – the date of his death.

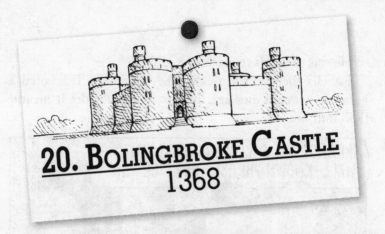

20. BOLINGBROKE CASTLE
1368

In 1349 the Black Death – a terrible plague – wiped out nearly half of the people in Britain. The lords and ladies in their castles had fewer peasants to do their work. But just because you were a lord or lady living in a castle didn't mean you could escape the plague.

Terrible Tale

Blanche of Lancaster was born at Bolingbroke Castle in 1345. When the Black Death arrived in 1349 she didn't catch it. She went on to marry John of Gaunt and in 1367 she gave birth to baby Henry who grew up to become King Henry IV. But Blanche never lived to see her son on the throne.

The Black Death may have arrived in England 1349, but it kept coming back. In 1368 it killed Blanche. She was just 23 years old.

HI. I'M BACK

Did you know?

The Black Death – or Bubonic Plague – was a painful
way to go. An Italian explained in his diary ...

> There appeared certain swellings in the groin
> and under the armpit, the victims spat blood, and
> in three days they were dead.

These swellings began to ooze with blood and pus.
Purple-black blotches appeared on the skin and you
smelled absolutely revolting. Mr Death was seen as
a skeleton in a black cloak who carried a scythe
that swept you away with a swishing stroke.

Swell – Spit – Smell – Swish. You were gone.

The piles of bodies grew like chopped straw
into a haystack. The corpses were loaded onto
carts, and dropped into pits – or, in Avignon in
France, thrown into the river.

Children were Mr Death's favourites when it
came to the swish.

Nowadays we know the real reason for this

If you are adult then you have had quite a
few diseases in your lifetime and built up a

'resistance'; children have had fewer diseases and have far less resistance. They die easily. Of course priests said the children probably got what they deserved. One explained . . .

> *It may be that children suffer heaven's revenge because they miss going to church or because they despise their fathers and mothers. God kills children with the plague – as you can see every day – because, according to the old law, children who are rebels (or disobey their parents) are punished by death.*

Has much changed?

The Legend

Bolingbroke Castle is haunted by a phantom hare, which local people say is a witch who was once held prisoner in the castle. If you go there and don't see it they'll tell you it's the usual story – hare today and gone tomorrow.

21. LOCHINDORB CASTLE
1371

There may have been some kind castle keepers who were cuddly and cute in their keeps. But there were more villains who used their power to bring pain to the peasants. Scotland was a dangerous place in the 1300s. If the plague didn't get you a wolf just might.

Terrible Tale

Robert the Bruce took over as leader when William Wallace died and he had himself crowned king.

Robert's greatest stroke of luck was that Edward I died soon after Robert came to the throne. He was left to face the feeble Edward II. The Scottish king defeated the English king at the Battle of Bannockburn in 1314 and won the right of Scotland to be free of English rule

Robert the Bruce had a great rival for the Scottish throne, John Comyn of Badenoch, who lived in a castle on an island in a loch (or lake). They made a deal – Bruce would have the crown but Comyn could have the lands. Seemed fair enough. But they fell out.

Bruce agreed to meet Comyn at the church of Greyfriars in Dumfries to make peace.

Unfortunately Comyn laughed at Bruce's complaints. Bad-tempered Bruce stuck his dagger in Comyn and that stopped him laughing.

Bloodstained Bruce rushed from the church. 'I'm afraid I've stabbed Comyn.' His friend, Kirkpatrick, said, 'Don't be afraid – I'll go and make sure.' Kirkpatrick went and finished off the dying man.

In 1371 King Robert II (Bruce's grandson) gave the castle at Lochindorb to his son Alexander, hoping it would calm down the wild child. It didn't work. Alexander became known as the 'Wolf of Badenoch'. He dumped one wife and went off with another. The Bishop of Elgin said he was wicked … so Alex rode out from Lochindorb and burnt not just Elgin Cathedral but also the monastery, parish church and hospital.

Did you know?

'The Wolf of Badenoch' had a nasty habit of hunting in the Rothiemurchus Forest. He set fire to parts of it to drive out the deer so he could kill them. He also enjoyed hunting outlaws in the same way.

Top Heartless Hunting Tips
1. *Pre-roast before skewering*

The Legend

When awful Alex caught a victim he locked them in the Lochindorb dungeon in a metre of icy water. If the prisoner stood up he would live – if he tried to sit down or fell asleep, he would drown. He was left there for two or three days. If he lived then he would be set free.

22. NORWICH CASTLE
1381

The Black Death made the peasants precious – there were so few left. They decided it was time to stand up to the lords in their castles. A new tax called the Poll Tax was unfair, the rebels said. A man called Wat Tyler led 'The Peasants' Revolt' in 1381 ... he met the king but ended up dead.

Terrible Tale

In Norfolk, the revolt was led by Geoffrey Litster, a weaver, and Sir Roger Bacon, a local lord who supported the revolting peasants.

Sir Robert Salle was in charge of the Norwich defences and met Litster outside the castle to make peace. The rebels killed him.

The people of the town then opened the gates to let the rebels in. They began looting buildings.

The Earl of Suffolk, inside the city, knew they'd kill him so he disguised himself and ran off to London. Other lords

THAT'S ME,
BISH AND BASH

were captured and forced to be servants to Litster.

The revolt in East Anglia was put down by the Bishop of Norwich. When he found out about it, the bishop marched south with eight foot soldiers and a small group of archers. More men joined him as he marched to meet the rebels.

He marched through Peterborough, where he beat the rebel rabble and executed any he could capture – even the ones who had taken shelter in the local abbey.

The bishop captured Norwich Castle then set off to track down the rebel leader, Geoffrey Litster.

Litster was caught and executed.

Did you know?

The bishop saved Norwich, but executing rebels without a fair trial was against the law. Did he care? No.

The Legend

Norwich Castle stands on a hill where a really ancient fort once stood. A legend says a king was once buried there along with his hoard of silver and gold.

23. PONTEFRACT CASTLE
1399

The peasant revolts against King Richard II failed. But when the lords revolted, the king was in danger. Deadly danger. The chief rebel was Henry Bolingbroke. He invaded England and Richard was thrown off the throne and locked away in Pontefract Castle. You can guess what happened next.

Terrible Tale

When Richard II was 29 years old he married Isabella of France who was just 7 years old ... weird.

The people of London gave Richard a camel as a present. His wife was given a pelican...

Once Richard was locked away in Pontefract in 1399 he was never seen alive again. One story says he was simply starved to death.

Did you know?

Pontefract Castle is an unusual case. It was not destroyed in war or by enemy action. It was destroyed by the locals. The people of Pontefract. Why would the people want to destroy their local castle?

In 1644, during the English Civil War, the Roundheads captured it from the Cavaliers. The people of Pontefract were sick and tired of armies attacking the castle. They pulled it down themselves so there'd be no more fighting in their town.

IT'S AN ASABO...
ANTISOCIAL ARMY
BEHAVIOUR ORDER

The Legend
Pontefract has the usual woman-in-grey ghost wandering around at night. More unusual, it has two ghostly children who play near the dungeon of the castle.

NO SIGHT OF THE CASTLE AT THE SITE OF THE CASTLE

HA HA

24. RADNOR CASTLE
1403

The people of Wales never really liked the kings of England ruling them and there were revolts all the time. At the end of the 1300s the biggest ever revolt was led by a Welsh hero called Owain Glyndwr. He won a lot of battles but he failed in the end.

SPOILER ALERT

Terrible Tale

It is said that history is written by the winners. Owain lost so the historians made him seem worse than he was. Take the story of Radnor Castle.

Owain's forces were said to have attacked it in 1403. They captured the sixty men inside. Owain then gave orders to hang all 60 of the men from the walls of the castle.

But he was spiteful and went further.

But is the story true? Human bones WERE accidentally disturbed when the church was repaired in 1843. And the skulls were piled separately to the skeletons. They had been piled in a mass grave. Owain's victims?

But now historians think the story of the massacre of the garrison is just a legend that never really happened.

It was said the castle keeper at Peterston-super-Ely fortress was beheaded after he surrendered to Owain.

The Legend

In the 1700s Thomas Pennant collected the stories of Owain that made him out as the chief hero of the Welsh. They say Owain's still alive. He is sitting in a cave playing chess with King Arthur, waiting for the day when the Welsh need a hero to save them. Does that sound a bit like the King Arthur legend ... again?

25. THREAVE CASTLE
1440

In 1422 Henry VI took the throne. He was 8 months old. He was weak in body and mind and claimed to hear angels singing. Strong nobles decided this was their chance to grab power and they fought 'The Wars of the Roses' for many years. In Scotland there was a child-king at the same time so the Scots suffered murder and misery too.

Terrible Tale

James II of Scotland was just nine years old. Sir William Crighton ruled the country for the lad.

He decided to use his power to get rid of some hated enemies – the Douglas family. Crighton invited two young Douglases to dinner in Edinburgh Castle. They arrived from their home in Threave Castle. They never returned. A chronicle said …

> *Young King James II greeted them with great joy and gladness.*

It's easy to be joyful and glad when you don't know what will happen next isn't it?

They had a rich feast which ended when Crighton had a bull's head placed on the table in front of the guests. 'A bull's head?' (you cry). 'What's that all about? (you cry some more.)

I can tell you (and stop your crying): the bull's head was the sign of a death sentence. (And it was pretty deadly for the bull too.) Crighton took the Douglas boys into the next room, gave them a quick 'trial' before having them beheaded in the courtyard.

Young James II was upset and probably called Regent Crighton the biggest party-pooper of all time. It was enough to put anyone off their dinner.

<u>Did you know?</u>

William Douglas of Threave wanted to take the crown from James II. Patrick MacLellan wanted to keep James on the throne. So William captured

Patrick, locked him away at Threave Castle and – you guessed it – murdered him.

THREAVE CASTLE

HACK HACK

Don't worry, James II took his revenge and it was very personal. James invited William to Stirling Castle, drew a knife and stabbed him in the neck. The king's guards finished him off and threw the corpse of William Douglas from a window.

STIRLING CASTLE

STAB STAB

THROW

The Legend
At Threave Castle you can't see ghosts ... but you can hear them chattering away.

26. POWDERHAM CASTLE
1455

The Wars of the Roses were in full flow by 1455 as the York family claimed the throne of feeble Henry VI from the Lancaster family.

Terrible Tale

While the York and Lancaster families scrapped for power, OTHER families used the war as an excuse to fight each other.

The Earl of Devon found himself fighting against his own cousins, the Courtenays of Powderham Castle. The families had squabbled for years because they both thought they should rule the county of Devon. The Earl decided to attack Powderham and paid 1,000 men to form an army. Men who fight for money are called 'mercenaries'.

The siege went on for two months. When friends of Powderham tried to battle through, the Duke of Exeter beat them and destroyed their villages. The battle was at a place called Clyst Heath. A lot of the Courtenay family died in the Wars of the Roses ... many of them being beheaded.

Did you know?

A hundred years later there was ANOTHER battle at Clyst Heath ... and this time it was far more cruel and bloody. The Cornish people were rebelling against King Edward VI's Tudor Prayer Book. Would YOU fight over a prayer book? No. How about a *Horrible Histories* book? Yes.

The king's forces arrived at Clyst Heath and captured 900 Cornish prisoners. The general in charge didn't want the problem of looking after the prisoners. The Cornish rebels were bound and gagged and helpless. He gave the order to his German mercenary troops.

KILL THEM ALL. CUT THEIR THROATS

How long did it take for a thousand men to cut 900 throats?

a) 900 minutes

b) 90 minutes

c) 10 minutes

The Legend

If you stay in Powderham Castle now you may be bothered by an evil black cat invading your bedroom. Why? Who knows? It's a moggy mystery.

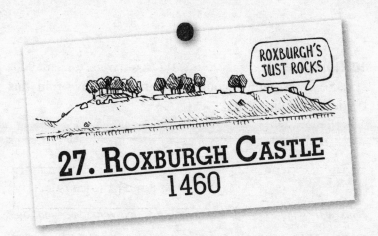

ROXBURGH'S JUST ROCKS

27. ROXBURGH CASTLE
1460

The days of castles were nearly done. A new weapon would soon make walls look weak as water. The new weapon was the cannon.

As the English squabbled among themselves in the Wars of the Roses, the Scots were also fighting one another. And they used those new cannons. Sometimes with horribly disastrous results.

Terrible Tale

If a Scottish gunner could write he may have told this tragical tale in his diary …

3 August 1460

This war stuff is a bit like football - you win some, you lose some. Today we won the battle but lost our captain, carried off the field injured. Mind you, we couldn't play football. King James II banned it - the miserable trout. He'll not be banning it now.

James II was always a great one for these new cannon things. He bought them from over in Flanders. And there was one other thing he was keen on … apart from banning football and using cannon. (That's two things.) He liked to attack English castles. His plan was to knock all their northern castles down while the English were fighting each other in those Rosy Wars.

So today we attacked Roxburgh. James stood by his favourite cannon, a monster he called 'The Lion'. He raised a hand and cried, "Fire!" The gunner lit the fuse. The fuse burned down. The gunpowder exploded … and blew the Lion apart. A great lump of metal sliced the King's leg off. He was soon dead.

Ah well, at least the lads will have a nice game of football once the castle's been captured.

Roxburgh Castle was captured two days after James II's accident. His widow, Queen Mary, had the castle destroyed.

Did you know?

Roxburgh had been captured by a Scottish army almost 150 years before in 1314. They were led by Lord Douglas and he had a daft plan. He disguised his men as cattle so they could creep up to the walls without being spotted. Daft? It worked.

The Legend

Go to Roxburgh now and you can see the ghost of James II charging around on horseback … a ghostly horse I guess.

Top 10 Castle Weapons

1. DISEASE WEAPON

1n 1347 the Tartar warriors attacked the
Italian traders in the fortified
stronghold of Kaffa. The
Tartars lobbed corpses that
had died of the plague
into the fortress.

2. TERROR WEAPON

When William The Conqueror attacked Alençon in France in 1048 he
took 34 prisoners. He paraded them in front of the town walls.
Then, as the people of Alençon watched, he had their hands and
feet cut off and lobbed over the wall.

3. GREEK FIRE

Records from the 1200s tell of "Greek fire" used by the Saracens against the Crusaders. A long tube on wheels was used to blow flames forward using large bellows. The sticky, flaming liquid burned down castles.

4. BATTERING RAM

A siege engine that originated in ancient times and was designed to break open the masonry walls of fortifications or splinter their wooden gates.

5. BOILING WATER

The legend of pouring boiling oil from the walls onto attackers is a fiction. Oil was too precious. They would pour boiling water.

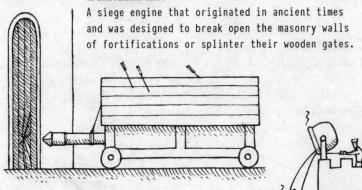

6. SIEGE TOWER

The tower was often on four wheels with its height roughly equal to that of the wall or sometimes higher. Archers would stand on top of the tower and shoot arrows into the fortification.

7. BATTERY TOWER

Took on a similar role to the siege tower, but mounted with cannon. These were built out of wood and mounted with siege artillery. Russian military engineer Ivan Vyrodkov built one in just one night during the Siege of Kazan in 1552.

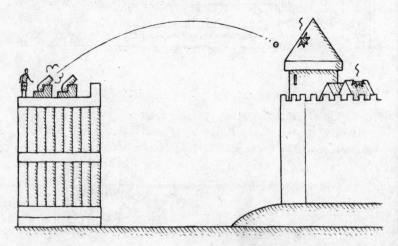

8. THE PETARD

An explosive device designed specifically for breaching gates and walls. The petard had to be placed directly against the surface of the fortress or in a tunnel under the walls. The name petard comes from an old French word meaning 'to break wind'.

9. THE ONAGER

A type of catapult that uses a torsional force, generally from twisting a rope, to store energy for the shot. Fired clay balls full of inflammable material.

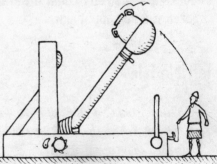

10. A TREBUCHET

A type of siege engine most frequently used in the Middle Ages. It is sometimes called a counterweight trebuchet because it worked on the principle of levers.

28. SANDAL CASTLE
1461

Back in England the leader of the York army – the Duke of York – marched up to fight the army of the Lancaster family. Children still sing about him.

Terrible Tale

> *Oh, the grand Old Duke of York, he had ten thousand men,*
> *He marched them up to the top of the hill, and he marched them down again.*
> *And when they were up they were up, and when they were down they were down.*
> *And when they were only halfway up they were neither up nor down.*

It was a bitter winter and the duke took his army of 6,000 men to Sandal Castle to shelter before the battle. It's a small castle and the men were cold, hungry and crowded.

A lookout spied a small troop of Lancaster soldiers in the valley below. You can imagine the York men would be glad to get out and do a little fighting.

So the Grand Old Duke of York led the charge down the hill – just like the nursery rhyme says. He didn't know that a larger army of Lancaster troops were hiding in the trees. The hidden army charged out and smashed the York army. The duke was chopped down. His head was cut off and taken back to the city of York and stuck on a pole.

The Legend

A small, yapping phantom terrier scares other much larger dogs away from Sandal Castle. If you touch it then the phantom fades away.

29. NOTTINGHAM CASTLE
1485

The Wars of the Roses came to an end in 1485 when the Yorkist King Richard III was beaten in battle by the Lancaster warrior, Henry Tudor. They fought at the Battle of Bosworth Field. But before the battle King Richard III stayed at Nottingham Castle.

Terrible Tale

Of course Nottingham Castle is famous for Prince John ... Earl of Nottingham. His brother, King Richard I, went off to fight in the Crusades and left John in charge. John turned Nottingham into a nest of traitors. They plotted against Richard I – John's own brother.

But Richard came home, and defeated John. He brought some of the catapults he'd used in the Crusades and broke into the castle. John begged for mercy. Richard said ...

NOT ONLY WILL I SPARE YOU BUT I WILL LET YOU RETURN TO THE CASTLE

THANKS BRUV

WHAT A MUG

Richard went back to the Crusades where he died and his brother became KING John. In the year 1212 John committed the most horrible act ever seen in Nottingham ... 'The massacre of the hostages'. It would have made headline news if there had been television news in those days.

28 WELSH BOYS TO BE EXACT. AND I AM GOING TO SHOW LLYWELYN WHAT I DO TO HIS PRECIOUS HOSTAGES IF HE REBELS

THEY ARE PUTTING ROPES AROUND THEIR NECKS

IT WON'T HURT THEM

THEY'RE BEING MADE TO CLIMB TO THE TOP OF THE WALLS

THAT WON'T HURT THEM EITHER. PASS ME A PEACH

THAT'S A VERY SMALL HOSTAGE

THE ONE ON THE END? IT'S A BOY. SON OF A TROUBLEMAKER CALLED MAELGWN. SEVEN YEARS OLD, I THINK

YOU ARE SIGNALLING WITH YOUR HAND AND...

YES, THE GUARDS ARE PUSHING THEM OFF THE RAMPARTS. NOW THAT WILL HURT A BIT, I IMAGINE. IT'S WHAT HAPPENS TO ANYONE WHO CROSSES KING JOHN OF ENGLAND.

NOW PASS ME A PEACH...

King John died of eating too many peaches.

Fast forward again to 1485 and Richard III left Nottingham Castle and died on the battlefield when Welsh weasel Henry Tudor defeated him. Richard was the last 'English' monarch to rule and took part in the last great charge of knights on a battlefield. The world was changing for knights and castles.

Henry Tudor became Henry VII and the first of the Terrible Tudors.

The Legend

At Nottingham you can hear rebel Roger Mortimer walking round his prison cell in the castle as he would have done before the traitor was executed in 1330 on the orders of Edward II.

Queen Isabella (the 'She-Wolf of France') can be heard howling, as she did when they dragged her boyfriend Roger Mortimer away to die.

30. STIRLING CASTLE
1520s

The Terrifying Tudors ruled in England while the Stuarts ruled in Scotland. Henry VII's daughter, Margaret, became Queen of Scotland when she married James IV of Scotland.

But that didn't mean there was peace between the two countries. The Northern castles were always nervous places to live. When would the other side attack? But it wasn't all war ...

Terrible Tale

The Scots (probably) invented golf. But they also had a sport that, strangely, you'd never see in the Olympic Games. It was called Hurley Hacket. It was fun to play but a bit horrible to prepare. Still, if you don't mind a bit of blood and don't mind being locked away for animal cruelty you can try it.

Hurley Hacket (or Summer Sledging.)

To play:

1. Take a dead horse. There were plenty of those around in the Middle Ages. Not so many today. Maybe a dead tea-tray would do. But if you do find a dead horse then boil its head till the flesh drops off.

2. Take the clean skull to 'Heading Hill' in Stirling. (It's full name was Be-heading Hill because that was the place where they gave chops to tops).

3. Use the skull as a sledge and slide down the grassy hill. (If you can't get to Stirling then a small hill like Mount Everest would do.) Or go to Calton Hill in Edinburgh, where young people also enjoyed this sport.

If you haven't got a dead horse (or 'hack') then you can't play Hurley Hacket. But you can play Hurley Haaky if you have a haaky skull – what's a haaky? It's a Scots word for a cow.

Did you know?

A champion at Hurley Hacket was King James V who liked this sort of sledging better than ruling the country.

James V became king at the age of one. When he grew older he kept control of the wild Highland clans by holding many of their chiefs as prisoners. He said ...

I have a list of 300 nobles that I can hang whenever I wish.

He was not a popular man – well, not with the 300 nobles on his hanging list.

James V hadn't the courage to lead his army against a full English force. He sent a leaderless army to fight and they were defeated. It was a killer shock. James, aged just 30, gave up on life, lay down on his bed and simply died. His throne passed to his daughter, Mary Queen of Scots, who was just six days old at the time. She would cause a lot of trouble for the English AND the Scots.

The Legend

The ghost of a woman in a pink silk dress stalks the area outside Stirling Castle. They say this is the ghost of Mary Queen of Scots. Maybe she is hoping to play Hurley Hacket like her dear, dead dad? She came to a messy headless end, just like the horses that gave the hurley skulls ... as you will see.

31. KIMBOLTON CASTLE
1536

By 1536 the monstrous Henry VIII was on the throne. He didn't build castles, he built palaces. But old castles like Kimbolton came in handy for packing away unwanted wives.

Terrible Tale

King Henry VIII had a daughter, Mary, with his wife Catherine of Aragon. But he wanted a son to take the crown when he died. All their other babies died young. The answer was to divorce Catherine and marry a younger wife.

Henry chose Anne Boleyn. But first he had to divorce Catherine. The head of the Catholic Church, the Pope, refused to allow Henry to divorce Cath so Henry divorced the Pope and made himself head of his own English church – the Protestant Church. He then married Anne.

What could he do with Catherine? Pack her off to the miserable Kimbolton Castle.

At Kimbolton she kept herself to one room (which she only left to go to the castle chapel). She dressed only in a scratchy hair shirt like a nun and fasted all the time.

Henry let her have a few visitors, but she was not allowed to see her daughter, Mary. Henry said,

YOU CAN LIVE IN A FINER PALACE AND SEE YOUR DAUGHTER IF YOU AGREE THAT ANNE BOLEYN IS THE RIGHTFUL QUEEN

Mary and Catherine refused his offer. So Catherine suffered in lonely Kimbolton. A couple of servants were there to care for her when she fell sick in January 1536.

I AM DOCTOR MIGUEL DE SA, THE QUEEN'S LOYAL SPANISH DOCTOR. SADLY SHE IS VERY SICK. SEE HERE?

I AM VERY SICK. I THINK I'VE BEEN POISONED

SOMEHOW — WE DON'T KNOW EXACTLY HOW — THE EVIL WOMAN ANNE BOLEYN MANAGED TO PLACE HER OWN WICKED SERVANTS HERE IN KIMBOLTON. THEY HAVE POISONED QUEEN CATHERINE AND ALL THE SKILLS I HAVE CANNOT HELP HER

Did you know?

Catherine died on 7 January. Her doctors examined her heart. It was black in colour. The Tudor doctors muttered, "poison". Modern doctors say it was probably cancer.

On the day Catherine was buried, the baby of her enemy, Anne Boleyn, died.

The Legend

As you might have guessed, Catherine of Aragon's ghost walks the gallery. But more horrible, a story says a young girl was thrown from the castle walls. Her ghost also haunts those walls.

32. BOLTON CASTLE
1537

Catherine of Aragon had been popular with the people of England. She was kind to the poor and a good Catholic. Henry VIII was hated by many people. He wanted to close the monasteries and make the monks homeless. It was the monks who cared for the poor. So a Catholic rebellion started in the North of England. It was known as 'The Pilgrimage of Grace.' Henry crushed it with his usual cruelty.

Terrible Tale

The Abbot of Jervaulx monastery was Adam Sedbar. He wasn't a ruthless rebel but he did love the Catholic Church. In 1536 he joined the Pilgrimage of Grace.

A Catholic peasant army started attacking towns in Yorkshire and Henry decided it was time to act. The leaders of the Pilgrimage would be rounded up and charged with treason. Of course they'd be found guilty and executed. Fair trial? Henry VIII didn't do 'fair' trials.

Adam Sedbar fled to Bolton Castle where Baron Scrope sheltered him. Henry's soldiers followed Sedbar, so the abbot fled to the hills to hide. They soon captured him and took him to the Tower of London.

He was hanged, drawn and quartered – that means his insides were cut out while he was still alive, his head cut off and his body was chopped into four pieces. The heads of the rebels were stuck on spikes over London Bridge as a lesson to anyone who fancied being a rebel.

Did you know?

Bolton Castle was torched and took years to repair. What do you think happened to Baron Scrope of Bolton Castle who had given the abbot shelter?

a) Hanged, drawn and quartered and his head stuck on a pole?

b) He was forgiven by Henry VIII?

c) He drowned himself in the castle duck-pond before Henry could execute him?

The Legend

In 1568 Mary Queen of Scots ran away from Scotland when her lords turned against her. She ran to England and begged Queen Elizabeth I to shelter her. Elizabeth locked cousin Mary away in different castles for 18 years. Mary spent some time in prison at Bolton Castle. Her ghost walks around the courtyard.

REALLY? APPARENTLY I ALSO HAUNT STIRLING CASTLE, BORTHWICK CASTLE, LOCH LEVEN CASTLE, CRAIGNETHAN CASTLE, FOTHERINGHAY CASTLE AND TUTBURY CASTLE. EITHER I GET AROUND A BIT OR YOU PEOPLE NEED TO GET A LIFE

33. HAUGHTON CASTLE
1541

Henry VIII was happy to see the families on the Borders of England and Scotland fighting each other. It stopped the Scots invading. In the lawless Borders all sorts of terrible things happened.

Terrible Tale

If the lord of Haughton Castle, Thomas Swinburne was ever accused of killing Archie Armstrong – a notorious clan chief – his confession may have looked like this…

> *20th day of March in the Year of Our Lord 1541*
>
> *I did not murder Archie Armstrong. I quite liked him, but his death was an accident. Sort of.*
>
> *Everyone knows that Archie was the biggest rogue to ride the Borders. He was head of the thieving, cattle-stealing, sheep-rustling, highway-robbing Armstrong clan.*

They didn't care who they hurt.

So I was pleased when I caught him alone one day and a troop of the King's soldiers arrested him.

We decided to lock him in my dungeon until he could be taken to Newcastle for a trial. I sat to dinner that night mightily satisfied. I had made Northumberland a little safer.

But as I sat to dinner a messenger arrived. I was called away to York. Of course I expected Armstrong to be there when I got back. But when I reached York a few days later I felt into my pocket and that's when I found... the key.

I had the only key to his cell. Of course I raced back from York Castle as fast as I could ... but I was too late. Armstrong was dead on the floor. He'd starved to death. There was a lump torn out of his arm ... just here ... where he'd tried to eat his own flesh to stay alive. A rope would have been so much quicker.

Sorry, Johnny.

Swinburne said that he rode so hard to save Archie his horse dropped dead at Durham, exhausted.

In 1541 the avenging Armstrong family almost captured Haughton Castle from Thomas Swinburne. Their raid scooped nine horses and goods worth £40 – equivalent to a rich man's yearly pay.

The Legend

For many years the ghost of Archie Armstrong haunted the castle until it was banished by a local vicar, using a black bible. The ghost returned to Haughton for a short time, while the bible was taken to London for a new cover. But, when the book was returned to Haughton, Archie's ghost was rarely seen again.

No one knows if there is a galloping ghost of the poor dead-tired horse.

34. EDINBURGH CASTLE
1573

Mary Queen of Scots was imprisoned in England. In Scotland the lords squabbled over the right to rule when she left. Sir William Kirkcaldy promised to look after Edinburgh Castle for Mary and keep out her enemies till she could come back with an army. But Sir William's enemies kept him trapped inside for two years from 1571 till 1573. Then they borrowed huge English guns from Berwick to batter down the walls. The diary of death was about to begin...

Terrible Tale

> *25 April 1573*
>
> *A trumpeter called to Kirkcaldy in the castle ... "Surrender or we fire our bloomin' big gun." Kirkcaldy turned to his men, "Raise a red flag to show we will never surrender."*

> *15 May 1573*
>
> *Thirty guns were aimed at the castle. Two could fire hundred-pound cannonballs, needing a crane to load them.*

17 May 1573

All the guns opened fire together. The castle guns fired back. In the quiet between the shots, screams could be heard from women in the castle.

> AIEEE. THEY'LL DIRTY ME WASHING.

23 May 1573

At last David's Tower with its guns and men fumbled down the cliffs to their doom.

> THANKS FOR DROPPING IN

28 May 1573

The attackers captured the main well and poisoned another well. Kirkcaldy was lowered over the walls in his armour.

> I WANT PEACE TALKS

> I DON'T. I WANT YOUR COMPLETE SURRENDER OR NOTHING

29 May 1573

The hundred defeated defenders, with their wives and children, marched out proudly, banners flying.

30 May 1573

But there was no happy ending for brave Kirkcaldy. He was dragged on a sledge to the market cross and hanged along with his brother.

> I'M ALL CHOKED UP

Did you know?

In 1603 Francis Maubray was locked in the castle and waiting to go on trial. For what? Just for plotting to kill King James VI. Lots of people wanted him dead. Guy Fawkes and the Gunpowder Plotters tried again two years later. Maubray tried to escape from Edinburgh Castle. He made bed sheets into a rope and climbed out of a window. The 'rope' snapped and he was smashed on the rocks below.

His crushed corpse was taken to court anyway. He was found guilty and his dead body was hanged, beheaded and cut into quarters. Don't worry. It probably didn't hurt.

The Legend

From time to time a drummer can be heard marching around the castle. It is a sure sign that some disaster is about to happen.

35. MUNCASTER CASTLE
1580

Not all castles had horribly historical tales of kings and queens and fights with foul foes. Sometimes ordinary people had terrible tales told about them. Even a jolly jester in Muncaster Castle.

Terrible Tale

Muncaster is one of Britain's most haunted castles. Tom Fool, the 16th century jester, is the most powerful force but he's rarely seen.

I SAY, I SAY, I SAY... AT MUNCASTER CASTLE THE JESTER TOM FOOL WAS ORDERED TO ACT AS EXECUTIONER

HE HAD THE AXE FACTOR

THE LORD'S DAUGHTER FELL IN LOVE WITH A LOCAL CARPENTER. THE LORD WAS FILLED WITH HORROR

A HAMMER HORROR

After the Battle of Hexham in 1464 King Henry VI fled to Muncaster Castle where Sir John Pennington gave him shelter. Henry gave Sir John a glass drinking bowl with a prayer for their good fortune... so long as the glass stayed unbroken. The glass is known as the 'Luck of Muncaster' and is still unbroken to this day. Not so lucky for Henry VI who was murdered in the Tower of London on the night of 21 May 1471. His ghost appears at Muncaster Castle in the room where he slept.

The Legend

Most Muncaster Castle hauntings happen in the Tapestry Room. Visitors hear footsteps, see the door handle turn and the door open ... when there is nobody there. A child is heard crying by the window and sometimes a lady is heard singing. Outside there's a White Lady who haunts the gardens and roads around Muncaster. She is believed to be the ghost of Mary Bragg, a girl murdered in the early 1800s on the road near the Main Gate.

36. FOTHERINGHAY CASTLE
1587

Mary Queen of Scots was a nuisance. The Catholics in England wanted her for their queen. A Catholic plotter called Babington said he would murder Queen Elizabeth I and set Mary Queen of Scots free. Mary said, 'Go ahead.' Elizabeth's spies told Elizabeth and so Mary had to die. She was a prisoner at Fotheringhay Castle. Her beheading was messy.

Terrible Tale

Ten Foul Facts about Mary's execution

1 Mary didn't know she was to die till the night before it happened. She stayed awake all night, writing letters and praying. It would have been difficult to sleep with the scaffold being hammered together in the great hall.

2 Mary's jailers refused to let her have a Catholic priest to pray with her. This was a bit spiteful. They gave her a Protestant who was still trying to convert her when she was

122

on the scaffold. She simply said, 'I've lived a Catholic, so I will die a Catholic.' This didn't stop him going on and on.

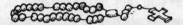

3 Mary's servants read a Bible story with her. It was the story of the good thief who died on the cross alongside Jesus. Mary heard it and said, 'That thief was a great sinner – but not such a great sinner as I have been.' Well, she HAD plotted against Elizabeth I.

4 The queen was not allowed to die in private. 300 people crowded into the hall to watch her execution. The scaffold platform was decorated in a pleasant shade of black and it made a very pleasant day out for the spectators. Some reported that she came into the hall 'cheerful and smiling.' So that was all right.

5 The axe-man asked her to forgive him – that was what executioners usually did. Mary did more and thanked him for, 'making an end to all my troubles'. She probably hoped this would help his aim. It didn't.

6 Mary was dressed in black until the time came for her to die. She took her dress off and was wearing a red petticoat underneath. She slipped on red sleeves and was all in red, so the blood wouldn't show. She wore a turban round her head to keep her hair out of the way of the axe. Her eyes were bound with a white cloth, trimmed in gold.

7 The axe-man's assistant held Mary's body steady while the axe fell. It missed the neck and cut into the back of her head. Her servants later said they heard her mutter, 'Sweet Jesus.' The second chop was a better shot but it still needed a bit of sawing with the axe to finish it off.

8 Traitors always had their severed heads held up for the spectators to look at. The executioner would cry out, 'May all traitors die this way.' Mary's executioner picked up the head by the hair ... but no one told him Mary was wearing a wig. The head slipped out and bounced over the scaffold. (Her real hair was short and grey.) The executioner was a bit upset and he forgot his lines. The Protestant priest was left to cry out, 'Let this be the end to all the Queen's enemies.'

9 Mary's pet dog, a Skye Terrier, had slipped into the hall under the cover of her skirts and was still hiding there when her head was lopped off. It finally came out, whimpering. It's said that the dog refused to eat and pined away until it died.

10 Mary's heart was removed and was buried in Fotheringhay Castle's grounds and hasn't been seen since. Mary asked to be buried in France. So, of course, she was buried in Peterborough, which is not quite the same thing. In 1612 her son, by then James I of England, had her coffin moved to Westminster Abbey where it is today.

Elizabeth I had sent a message to Mary's jailer telling him it would be better if he could quietly murder Mary. It may have been better if he had.

Mary's body was taken away to be mummified while her blood-stained clothes were burned. When her body was moved to Westminster Abbey - it was buried near the tomb of her enemy, Elizabeth I. Of course James made sure Mary's tomb was bigger than killer-queen Elizabeth's.

The Legend

At Fotheringhay, the Scottish national flower, the thistle, grew. People said the thistles sprang from the tears of Mary Queen of Scots.

THISTLE BE WHERE HER TEARDROPS FELL

37. LANCASTER CASTLE
1612

By the 1600s, castles were still useful as prisons. They were often cold and damp places. People died just from being in prison. Especially if they were old and weak when they were locked away.

Terrible Tale

Lancaster Castle was the prison where the Pendle witches were locked up and put on trial in 1612.

NOT REALLY. MOTHER DEMDIKE HAD ACCUSED A VILLAGER OF STEALING. SO THE VILLAGER ACCUSED MOTHER DEMDIKE AND ALIZON OF WITCHCRAFT. ALIZON PANICKED IN THE WITNESS BOX

IT'S TRUE — MY GRANDMOTHER WAS A SERVANT OF THE DEVIL. I SAW HER CHARM A CAN OF MILK SO THAT A QUARTER POUND OF BUTTER APPEARED IN IT

OH COME ON. MOTHER DEMDIKE SAT IN HER HOUSE WITH ONLY ONE THIN DRESS TO WEAR. SHE WAS EIGHTY YEARS OLD AND COMPLETELY BLIND. WOULD THE DEVIL TREAT HIS SERVANTS SO BADLY, ALIZON?

WELL, HE DID

JENNET DEVICE WAS JUST NINE YEARS OLD BUT THE COURT BELIEVED HER TALES ABOUT THE WITCHES IN HER VILLAGE

MY MOTHER HAD A PARTY ON GOOD FRIDAY WHEN ALL GOOD PEOPLE SHOULD BE IN CHURCH. SHE'S A WITCH

In 1633 Jennet herself was accused of being a witch ... by a 10-year-old boy. In the end he said he was lying. But Jennet was not set free until she had paid for the cell and the food she'd had while she was in Lancaster Castle jail.

Between the 1400s and the 1700s over 500 men and women were hanged for being witches.

The Legend

King James I was on the throne at the time of the Lancaster witchcraft trials. He believed there were several black-magic plots to kill him before he came to the English throne. He went along to secretly watch them being tortured.

38. WARWICK CASTLE
1628

King Charles I came to the throne in 1625. The English people wanted to rule the country through Parliament. Charles I wanted to rule. In the end the king and his lords (the Royalists) went to war with Parliament and the people (the Roundheads). But life (and death) went on in the great castles like Warwick.

Terrible Tale

The Earls of Warwick have been so important in English history. Back in 1431 the Earl of Warwick was in charge of the trial of Joan of Arc. He made sure she was burned to death in the marketplace at Rouen in northern France.

The Warwick earls were big in the Wars of the Roses too – in 1469 the earl locked away King Edward IV.

An Earl of Warwick was even part of the 1605 Gunpowder Plot. Some of the plotters waited at Warwick Castle to hear if Guy Fawkes had blown up Parliament. When they heard he'd failed they stole horses from the stables at Warwick to help in their escape.

Some Earls of Warwick died horribly. In 1628 Ralph Heywood was a top servant to the earl, Fulke Greville. He was sure he would be left a lot of money in the earl's will when he died. Then he discovered he wasn't. Heywood was so furious he took a knife and stabbed the earl. He then turned the knife and stabbed himself to death.

The earl may have lived but his doctors treated the wounds by packing them with pig fat. The pig fat turned bad and made the wounds poisonous. Earl Fulke Greville died in terrible pain four weeks after the attack.

In 1153, the wife of the 2nd Earl of Warwick was defending the castle from King Henry II. She was told that her husband had died in battle - that was a lie. So she gave up. When he heard that his wife had handed over the castle, the earl really did die from the shock.

The Legend

Murdered Fulke Greville's ghost is said to haunt the tower in which he lived.

HE'S ALIVE, HE'S DEAD. I'VE GOT THE CASTLE, I'VE LOST THE CASTLE. THEN HE'S ALIVE AND DEAD AGAIN. EMOTIONAL ROLLER COASTER OR WHAT?

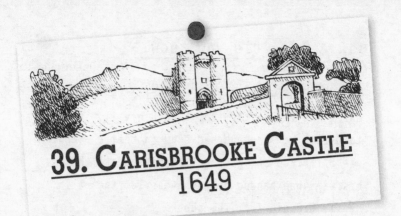

39. CARISBROOKE CASTLE
1649

The Roundheads won the English Civil War and King Charles I was made a prisoner in Carisbrooke Castle.

Terrible Tale

Charles I was locked in Carisbrooke for almost a year. Charles made several escape attempts but they all failed. He also tried to smuggle secret messages to friends. The messages said, 'Send the Scottish Army to set me free.'

The Roundhead leader, Cromwell was furious. He said this was treason against the English people… and the punishment for treason should be death. A trial decided Charles should be executed.

Charles stepped onto the scaffold and prepared to say some famous last words … but what were they? As he took off his jewels and handed them to the bishop beside him he said,

REMEMBER

Brilliant. What a dramatic last word. But Charlie had to go and spoil it. After a few moments of silent prayer he took off the cloak and put his neck on the block. The executioner brushed Charles's hair to the side to give him a clean cut. Charles said,

WAIT FOR THE SIGN

What a let-down. 'Wait for the sign.' What sort of last words are they? They could be the last words of a policeman trying to stop a steamroller at a crossroads.

Anyway, Charles stretched out an arm, the axe fell and cut off the head cleanly. The crowd surged forward and some dipped handkerchiefs in the blood.

THE BLOOD OF AN EXECUTED MAN IS A GOOD LUCK CHARM

NOT FOR HIM

Charles' two youngest children were kept in Carisbrooke, and Princess Elizabeth, aged 14, caught a cold and died there.

The Legend

Carisbrooke Castle is haunted by two ghosts. One is a grey woman in a long cloak, walking four small dogs on chains. The other is the ghost of a young girl who drowned in the castle well. Her face can be seen if you look down the well. Who'd have thought it? Well, well, well.

40. SKIBO CASTLE
1650

It may have been the English Civil War but Scotland was mixed up in it too and lords there took different sides. So did ladies.

Terrible Tale

In the 1640s the Earl of Montrose fought to keep Scotland for Charles II. But then he was captured. His enemies treated him dreadfully. Montrose was dressed in peasant rags, tied to an old horse and led south. When the prisoner reached Skibo Castle the lady of the house decided Montrose should have the best seat at the dinner table.

Instead General Holbourn, the commander of the guards, took that seat. The lady told the general to move.

He refused. What did she do? She picked up a steaming leg of roast lamb and a report says ...

> *She gave him such a great blow on his head, it knocked him off his chair.*

... and Montrose got to sit at the best seat.

The soldiers at the dinner table were scared this might be part of a rescue attempt on Montrose. It wasn't. The lady just said it was her dining room so her guests had to do what SHE said.

The mutton went back on the table and everyone ate it quietly. Tender meat but tough lady.

Did you know?

A leg of lamb may have given Montrose some respect. But, after he was executed, it was a leg of Montrose that was stuck on a pole over a castle in Scotland. When King Charles II returned as king 11 years later, Montrose's enemy was executed at the same spot.

The Legend

A legend tells the story of a young girl who was murdered by a gardener of Skibo Castle. He hid her body in the castle. While repairs were taking place, years later, a skeleton was found behind a wall in the building. Local people believed it was the skeleton of the murdered girl. Some guests of the castle have said they've seen the ghost of the young girl dressed in white wandering around.

The White Lady now drifts through the castle corridors, wailing and screaming.

41. CHEPSTOW CASTLE
1680

There was a king back on the throne. Charles II. Many castles had been smashed by the Roundheads in the English Civil War and it wasn't worth patching them up. The lords would start building fine country houses – stately homes – instead. But the old castles still had tales to tell.

Terrible Tale

Charles II was known as 'The Merry Monarch'. Well, he spent a lot of money on having a good time. The poor still starved in the streets but that didn't stop Cheerful Charlie Two having fun.

He wanted to forget the Civil War and all the fighting …. EXCEPT for the men who had signed his dad's death warrant. THEY would pay with their lives. They were hunted down.

Henry Marten was one of the men who sent Charles I to the executioner's axe. Even before Charles I was executed he was one of the people who wanted an end to royalty.

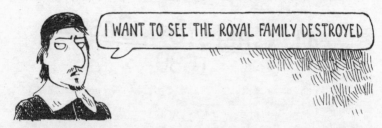

I WANT TO SEE THE ROYAL FAMILY DESTROYED

He thought all humans should be treated the same. We are all level ... so his group was known as the 'Levellers'. He almost got his way when Charles I's head was level with the ground.

Charles II sentenced 10 of his father's killers to be hanged, drawn and quartered. Henry Marten was spared that terrible death ... but was locked away in Chepstow Castle till he died in 1680. How did he die?

a) A royal assassin sneaked into Chepstow and stabbed him.

b) He was walking along the walls and fell off.

c) He choked to death while eating his supper.

Answer (c)

Did you know?

In 1638 the Leveller John Lilburne was punished for saying there should be no king or queen. He was stripped to the waist and his hands were tied to the back of the cart. An executioner lashed the prisoner with his three-strand, knotted whip. It was said that Lilburne received 500 lashes along the way, making 1,500 stripes to his back during the two-mile walk.

A report said ...

> *His back swelled almost as big as a penny loaf with the bruises of the knotted cords.*

All because, like Henry Marten, he said ...

NO SINGLE MAN IS WISE ENOUGH TO RUN THE WHOLE COUNTRY

The Legend

A cave under Chepstow Castle was once explored by a man who said he'd seen King Arthur and his knights lying there asleep. He ran away after making noises which made the knights stir.

42. DERRY CASTLE
1688

When Charles II died, his brother James II took the throne. But James was a Catholic and not popular. He was chased out of the country by the Protestants. He decided to get his throne back by landing in the north of Ireland then invading. But it didn't go to plan.

Terrible Tale

King James II landed in Ireland and was supported by Dublin Catholics. The Catholic army approached Derry – led from behind by the elderly Earl of Antrim who followed in a luxury coach.

The Catholic army expected the town to surrender quietly but when they were just 50 metres from the town gates a group of 13 Protestant apprentice boys closed the gates and locked them. The Siege of Derry had begun.

When King James himself arrived to command the siege it is the Protestant cry that is remembered to this day …

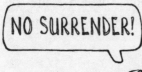

NO SURRENDER!

The new king, William, finally arrived to help Derry on 28th July 1689 – after siege had lasted 105 days.

The Catholics were defeated and jumpy James II fled to France. Was he grateful for the way his supporters had suffered to fight for him? Jim said ...

I BLAME THE IRISH CATHOLICS FOR MY DEFEAT

Nice man.

Did you know?

At the Siege of Derry the defenders were starving. The attackers were allowing some of their cows to graze near walls. The defenders rushed out to capture a cow. They killed 300 attackers ... but failed to capture a single cow.

I KNOW HISTORY CAN BE HORRIBLE BUT I DIDN'T EXPECT IT TO BE DAFT AS WELL

MOO

Someone in the hungry town then suggested an experiment. They took one of the last remaining cows inside Derry. The cow was to be tied to a stake and then burned alive. A sort of steak at the stake. The idea was that her cries would then attract other cows outside to rush to her rescue.

Fortunately the cow got loose from the flames and escaped.

The Legend

There is a story that James II fled from the Battle of the Boyne and whinged to an old woman who had the perfect answer ...

43. URQHART CASTLE
1692

James II was defeated. But still the Scots wanted the Stuart family on the throne. The English were worried. What if the Scots started a war and used their castles to fight the English? They began to knock down important castles like Urquhart. In 1692 it was smashed. But didn't disappear from history. For Urquhart stands on the shore of Loch Ness, and there are reports of a terrible monster that lives in the waters.

Terrible Tale

In 1933 people began to report a strange creature in Loch Ness, Scotland – and start a monster hunt that has gone on ever since. Urquhart Castle, they said, was the best place to see the creature.

Then World War Two started in 1939. In 1941 an Italian newspaper reported that the bombing of Scotland was so heavy, the Loch Ness Monster was killed by a direct hit. (The Italians said they'd made a messy of Nessie ... but the newspapers were lying).

Did you know?

Urquhart Castle has the ruins of a dovecote ... a home for doves. There were three reasons for keeping doves. Which three of the following?

1 For their eggs
2 For eating
3 For their singing
4 For their poo
5 For cat food

Answer:
1, 2 & 4. The poo could be used to spread on the gardens to make vegetables grow better.
Coo, I bet you didn't guess that.

WHO NEEDS VEGETABLES

The Legend

When the 1930s monster reports started then old legends were remembered.

One legend said that in AD 580 a saint called Columba was the first person to meet the famous Loch Ness Monster. He defeated it, naturally. (Sadly he didn't have a video camera with him because they hadn't been invented. If he had then he could have made a fortune from selling the recording.)

YOU WERE SNATCHED AWAY IN THE JAWS OF NESSY

THANKS FOR MY RESCUE, THAT COULD HAVE BEEN MESSY

Some legends record that the monk died in Nessie's jaws and Columba brought him back to life.

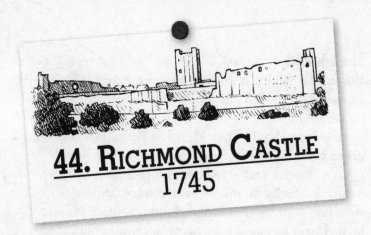

44. RICHMOND CASTLE
1745

James II was too old to invade England again. But rebel Scots supported his grandson, Bonnie Prince Charlie. The Scots attacked England in 1715 and again in 1745. They lost in the end but castles in the North of England were filled with soldiers again. Castles like Richmond.

Terrible Tale

There is a story of secret underground passages between the castle and Easby Abbey, a few miles away. Underground tunnels are a great idea for a castle. If the enemy surrounds you in a siege you can use the tunnels to get in and out with food.

It is said that castle soldiers in the 1745 Scottish rebellion discovered the entrance to a narrow passage. Was this the secret tunnel to Easby?

Who was brave enough to go into the dank and dark hole to see where it led? They sent down a little drummer boy because he could fit in easily.

The boy was told to play as he marched underground so the soldiers could follow the drumming from above. The boy marched under the ground. The soldiers followed above.

Then ... disaster. A mile from the abbey the drumming stopped. The boy was never seen again ... but it is said you can still hear the distant drums rattle below the ground. A stone now marks the spot where he fell silent.

You know you are posh when you have your own private toilet. Richmond Castle has the 'Gold Hole Tower'. In it there were rooms with a wooden seat over a hole. You sat, you pooed and it fell into the moat below. But the ones at Richmond were only to be used by the earl and his family. A private toilet. You don't get any posher than that.

The Legend

You may have heard this one somewhere before … under the keep of the castle, deep underground, is a secret room where King Arthur sleeps until Britain needs him.

That sleeping army gets around a bit doesn't it? Restless sleepwalkers maybe?

45. LOWTHER CASTLE
1784

Scotland and England were at peace again. Castles were still useful as prisons and as homes for landowners. In the 1691 Lowther Castle was rebuilt to make a fine home for the Earl of Lonsdale. He dropped the name 'castle' and called it Lowther Hall. But it could be as creepy as any castle and just the place for dark and dirty deeds.

Terrible Tale

❀ James Lowther was lord of Lowther castle. He is remembered as 'Wicked Jimmy'. Why? I am glad you asked and I will tell you.

❀ In 1784 James took over the castle. He was married to Mary but had lots of girlfriends.

My lovely new wife

Spares

❀ And then he fell in love with the daughter of one of the farmers on his lands. He was really happy. Mary probably wasn't.

❀ Then tragedy struck. The farmer's daughter died. James wept. He couldn't bear to be without her. So he had her put to bed in his bedroom. Dead. He ate meals with her corpse sat next to him.

❀ Of course her body started to go mouldy and smelled terrible. The servants complained. So she was put in a glass coffin and the coffin was put in a cupboard. The pong was sealed in but he could still look at her. Yeuch.

❀ After seven weeks she was finally buried in Paddington Cemetery near Wicked Jimmy's London home.

Did you know?

In 1792 in London Jimmy got into an argument with an army captain. They decided to have a duel to sort it out. That was how a gentleman ended an argument.

They both fired. They both missed. They shook hands. The end.

The Legend

Sir James returned to Lowther where he fell into a deep gloom and died on 24 May 1802. It is said that his coffin swayed over the open grave at his funeral and the mourners heard a knocking noise coming from inside. Some stories even say his angry spirit leapt from its coffin and tried to strangle the people at the graveside.

Sir James' ghost appears when the moon is full on 24 May. Wicked Jimmy can be seen sitting on a carriage, riding madly through the parkland, as he whips his ghastly, ghostly, shabby horses into a wild gallop.

SHABBY? THE CHEEK

46. DOVER CASTLE
1803

It seemed as if castles would never be used for defence again. Then Britain went to war with the French and their emperor, Napoleon. The British were worried Napoleon might invade so some of the castles around the coast were turned into strongholds again.

THAT SHOULD KEEP THEM OUT

Terrible Tale

After his victory at Hastings in 1066, William the Conqueror built a timber castle then a stone one at Dover. From then on Dover Castle was used as a fortress until 1958.

Why wasn't Dover Castle wrecked like others in the Civil War? In August 1642, most people in Dover were Roundheads. The Cavaliers were inside Dover Castle. The Dover people climbed the cliffs, surprised the soldiers inside and captured the castle with hardly a sound. Not even a cannon cracking the walls. That's why it's one of the largest castles in England.

In 1790s, during the wars against Napoleon, Dover Castle's defences were made stronger again. More gun posts were added, and the roof of the keep was taken off so that heavy cannon could be used from the top.

Tunnels were dug 50 metres below ground where soldiers could live, ready to attack if the French crossed the English Channel. There were over three miles of tunnels. Sadly the tunnels were dripping with damp and sometimes collapsed. By 1803 there were 2,000 soldiers living there, in the only underground army camp ever built in Britain.

The Legend

Visitors and staff have heard the sound of drumming coming
from the castle walls and some even say they have seen a
headless figure walking along them late at night. This ghost
is said to be Sean Flynn, a 15-year-old drummer boy.

Sean had been sent from the castle to the town of Dover
late one night to do some shopping. But two savage soldiers
had heard that Sean was carrying a lot of money. They
jumped on him. Sean tried to fight them off, but one mighty
blow from a sword took off his head. Now he's back to haunt
the castle.

47. CARDIFF CASTLE
1831

In 1825 the first passenger steam trains were running. It was part of the changing world we call the Industrial Revolution. Coal and iron were kings in Wales. But the workers stayed poor. Castles were not a lot of use except as places where criminals could be executed. Criminals AND innocent people were hanged outside the ancient walls.

← INSERT PERSON HERE

Terrible Tale

The Welsh iron workers didn't take the rich and bullying iron masters without a fight.

They wanted to protest against the dreadful conditions they had to live in. Tiny houses crammed together, disease and filth everywhere. The town of Merthyr Tydfil was packed with 22,000 people. Twenty-five years before there had only been 7,000. No wonder the iron workers wanted things to change.

In fact some died fighting for change. Men like Dic Penderyn ...

BETH YW'R SGÔR?
Find out in our 167-page rugby section

PLUS. YUM SCRUM. PERFECT RUGBY RECIPES TO TACKLE

Dic dies declaring 'I didn't do it.'

PENDERYN

Saturday 13th August 1831 was the last day for Richard Lewis – commonly known as Dic Penderyn.

He was hanged at St. Mary's Street, outside Cardiff Castle in front of a large crowd.

Dic was part of the Merthyr Riots back in May.

The iron-workers of Merthyr went on a march to get a better wage and to try and get the vote.

They marched into Merthyr and ransacked houses and robbed them.

One man in the crowd denied this. The man, known as Huw, said, 'We weren't robbers. The law officers had taken away our furniture because we were in debt. We were just taking them back.'

The iron workers went on to raid the courtroom, steal the court records and burn them in the streets.

Huw continued, 'There was no need to send in the army. They shot 24 of the workers dead.'

But 16 soldiers were also wounded and that's what led to the trials. 28 men and women put on trial.

They all ended up being sentenced to transportation to Australia. But for some reason Dic was sentenced to hang. Penderyn was found guilty of stabbing a soldier. But even the soldier said he couldn't identify Penderyn as the man who stabbed him.

It's said that the two men who accused Penderyn weren't even at the riot. They were two hairdressers. But Dic had just had an argument with them. They hated him.

Still he died bravely. Dic Penderyn, hands tied behind his back, was led onto the scaffold by a minister of the chapel.

Dic called 'O Arglwydd, dyma ganwedd.' Our Welsh readers will know that means, 'Oh Lord, here is injustice.'

The hangman placed a white bag over Penderyn's head and tied his feet. He pulled the lever and there was a gasp from crowd.

As the man Huw said, 'Dic Penderyn – a Welsh martyr.'

Poor Dic was only 23 years old and he was probably innocent.

Forty years after the hanging a man called Ieuan Parker confessed on his deathbed that he was the one who stabbed the soldier all those years ago.

Dic is remembered as a hero of the iron workers. But in fact Dic was a miner.

Did you know?

In 1679 two priests, John Lloyd and Philip Evans, were accused of preaching a Catholic service in Protestant Cardiff. The main witness against them was an elderly woman ... who had been paid £50 to say she'd seen them.

The judge found them guilty then told them to report back to the court in three months' time to hear their fate. Plenty of time to run away then? But that was the amazing thing. They swore to wait till three months had passed and kept their word. Philip Evans was brought the news of his death sentence while he was playing tennis near St. John's Church in Cardiff. When he heard the news he said,

WHAT HURRY IS THERE? LET ME FIRST FINISH MY GAME

He was sentenced to be hanged, drawn and quartered at Cardiff Castle. He heard the news and sang and played the harp in his cell. He stood on the scaffold, with the rope around his neck and said,

THIS IS THE BEST PULPIT ANY MAN CAN PREACH FROM

Then they butchered him and John Lloyd horribly.

The Legend

Robert, Duke of Normandy, was imprisoned by his brother, King Henry I, from 1106 until 1134. He spent his last eight years in Cardiff. There is a story that says the bridge over the River Taff in Cardiff is haunted by a grey lady called Sarah. She is waving towards the castle, looking for Duke Robert ... the love of her life. But he won't see her waving. When he was put in Cardiff Castle Duke Robert had his eyes plucked out.

MAYBE YOU SHOULD THROW A ROCK

48. BAMBURGH CASTLE
1902

By the 1900s some castles had been knocked down to make way for grand houses. Others were rebuilt to be comfortable homes or for tourists to visit.

Terrible Tale

Bamburgh Castle was bought by Lord Armstrong in 1894. It had been a fortress on the borders of Scotland since the days of the Ancient Britons. It had been fortified by the Saxons in AD 590 then destroyed by Viking raiders in 993. The Normans rebuilt it and it was besieged by King William II. In the Middle Ages the Scots attacked it and it became the first castle ever to be defeated by the use of cannons.

But no one cared for it and by the days of Queen Victoria it had crumbled and collapsed.

Then along came Lord Armstrong who wanted to turn it into a home for himself and houses for the poor. Local people were shocked.

It cost the Lord Armstrong £1 million to restore the castle. But maybe the locals had the last laugh. The new castle was finished in 1902 but Lord Armstrong never got to see it because he carelessly died in 1900. Well, he was 90 years old and as crumbly as the old castle.

Did you know?

The castle has been used by filmmakers to make movies many times. You can see Bamburgh in a dozen films from 'Robin Hood' to 'Elizabeth I' to Shakespeare's 'Macbeth'. (Not one of those characters went near Bamburgh Castle. Ever. But it looks good on film.)

The Legend

Bamburgh is the home of the legend of the Laidley Worm … a 'Worm' being a monster dragon.

Princess Margaret's mother, the queen of Northumbria, died. Margaret's brother, Childewynd, was away at the crusades. Her father said he planned to marry again.

Margaret waited at the gates of the castle to greet her new stepmother. One of the knights who rode beside the new queen saw Margaret and said she was the most beautiful woman in the land. The stepmother was a wicked witch – they usually are in fairy tales – and turned Margaret into the hideous Laidley Worm. She'd stay that way, the witch said, till Childewynd kissed it. The worm ate everything in sight.

The people were panicked. A wise man told them to feed the worm seven cows each day (a magic number) and send for Childewynd to sort it.

He returned to slay the worm but the worm cried:

Lay down your sword, unbend your bow,
And give me kisses three;
For though I am a poisonous worm,
No harm I'll do to thee.

You guessed the rest? Childewynd kisses the worm. Margaret is Margaret again.

Wynd went to the castle, touched the queen with the branch of a rowan tree (witches can't bear that) and she shrivelled up, till she became a huge ugly toad. She croaked and she hissed, and then hopped away down the castle steps.

Wynd and Margaret lived happy ever after.

49. DUBLIN CASTLE
1916

By the 1920 some people in southern Ireland were rebelling against the British ruling them from London. The old castle at Dublin was a battle site again.

Terrible Tale

In 1916 the rebels marched on Dublin. The rebels were outnumbered. When the fighting started the British army had three times as many men as the Irish. By the end of a week they had twenty times as many.

The rebels were cruelly killed by better weapons. They dug trenches in St. Stephen's Green Park. But those trenches were overlooked by the tall Shelbourne Hotel and rebels were machine-gunned from the windows.

The rebels stole workmen's carts to build barricades – when a harmless workman tried to take his cart away they shot him in the head.

An unarmed policeman at Dublin Castle asked them politely to leave. They shot him in the head. Ordinary people of Dublin shared the suffering of the rebels.

* A nun was killed shutting a convent window
* A young girl was killed as she stood in her door watching the fighting
* One man raised his hand to wave to a friend and was shot dead by British soldier who thought he was going to throw a bomb

All over central Dublin, the dead were buried in back gardens.

Did you know?

In 1185 Prince John arrived in Dublin and he was trouble. His lords made fun of the Irish chiefs. What did they do?

a) pull their ponytails
b) pull their beards
c) pull their helmets off

The Legend

Conor O'Devany was a Franciscan friar and bishop. In 1612, aged nearly 80 years old, he was accused of treason.

His punishment was to be publicly hanged in Dublin, have his guts pulled out before he was dead and then be cut into quarters.

The large Catholic crowd felt sorry for him, of course, but they pushed and jostled each other to get scraps of his clothing (or dip cloths in his blood). They didn't just do this after he was dead – they did it while he was being executed.

THAT'S REVOLTING

50. TOWER OF LONDON
1941

Of all the castles in Britain the most popular is the Tower of London. It has millions of visitors each year. They come to see the Crown Jewels and the place where so many horribly historical acts of torture and execution happened. Maybe they hope to see one of the ghosts. Not many know it was still being used for executions in World War Two.

Terrible Tale

The last person to be executed at the Tower was German spy Josef Jakobs who was shot on 15 August 1941.

In 1940 Joseph had been made an officer in the German army. Then they discovered he had a criminal past – he'd been flogging fake gold. He was offered a job as a spy and agreed to fly over Britain and drop in a parachute.

He was given a little training but he was never taught to parachute. His first jump was when he was dropped over England and (surprise, surprise) when he landed he broke his ankle. Two farmers spotted him and the Home Guard (or Dad's Army) arrested him.

There was no doubt he was an enemy spy. He was caught still wearing his German flying suit, he had £498 in British money, forged papers, a radio set, and ... the big giveaway ... a German sausage.

Jakobs was found guilty of spying and sentenced to death. He was a soldier in the German Army so he had to die like a soldier – shot by a firing squad, not hanged like the other spies who'd been caught.

He was taken to the Tower, he was sat, blindfolded, in a chair (because of his broken ankle) and shot eight times.

The blood-stained history of the Tower had one last victim.

Did you know?

From 1250 there was a Royal Menagerie at the Tower. King Henry III had a polar bear and the people of London loved it when the bear went fishing in the River Thames.

DO I REALLY HAVE TO SWIM IN THAT?

In 1254, the keepers of the Tower were ordered to pay for the building of an elephant house at the Tower.

I WANTED CURTAINS

Later lions were kept in the area known as Lion Tower. Over the years the kings and queens received animals as gifts like three leopards from Frederick III, the Holy Roman Emperor.

DO WE GET A LEOPARD TOWER, HMM?

In 1393 Richard II was given a camel and his wife given a pelican.

CALL ME HUMPTY AGAIN AND I'LL GET MY FRIEND HERE TO PECK YOU

In the 1700s the zoo was open to the public. It cost three half-pence to get in. Or what ELSE could you pay to get in?

a) you could hand over a cat or dog to be fed to the lions
b) you could scrub the floors in the White Tower
c) you could brush the lion's mane

SEEMS HARSH

Answer: (a)

A bit rough on your cat ... and a bit woof on your dog.

By 1828 there were over 280 animals and at least 60 different types. The last animals left in 1832, and went to Regent's Park Zoo. Why? Because one of the lions bit a soldier.

The Legend

Anne Boleyn was beheaded in 1536 when her husband, Henry VIII, grew tired of her. She haunts the chapel where she is buried, and has been seen walking around the White Tower carrying her head under her arm. Well, where else would she carry it?

IN A HEAD-CASE

EPILOGUE

Most castles are ruined these days. But they are still popular places to visit.

It isn't the dry and tumbling stones that people go to see. They go to see where people from the past lived and hear the strange stories that are told.

A lot of those tales are quite horrible. We human beings seem to like being shocked by dreadful deeds, not sweet stories.

The world will never change. We don't want happy history, do we? We all want horrible histories.

SITE OF GRISLY MURDER

GIFT SHOP ➡

INDEX